A GIFT OF GRATITUDE

A COMMUNITY BOOK PROJECT

DONNA KOZIK, LEAD EDITOR

WWW.COMMUNITYBOOKPROJECT.COM

A Gift of Gratitude:
A Community Book Project

Donna Kozik, lead editor

Gregory Hoffmaster, cover designer

Limits of Liability and Disclaimer of Warranty

Warning – Disclaimer

Acknowledgments

I give great thanks to so many people for their help in putting together this third edition of "The Community Book Project!" My gratitude and appreciation go to Gregory Hoffmaster for help with proofreading and cover design. Thank you to Clark Kenyon for interior formatting and Darian Crum for help with the directory of our causes. Thank you also to Maggie Ortiz, my accidental life coach, and Teresa and Brad Castleman for constant support and cat pictures. Finally, heaps of love go to all the cheerleaders in the Business Authors Association who left encouraging words on our Facebook page.

I am grateful for you!

~ Donna Kozik, lead editor

About Donna Kozik

USA Today, *Wall Street Journal* and Amazon bestselling author Donna Kozik shows people how to write a book fast and easy to use as a "big business card" for themselves and their businesses.

She does this with her signature online program, Write a Book in a Weekend, which she has conducted over 70 times in 10 years, showing thousands of people how to get a short and powerful book done in just two days.

Find out more at www.MyBigBusinessCard.com and download a free book planner at www.FreeBook-Planner.com.

To contact Donna directly, email her at Donna (at) MyBigBusinessCard (dot) com.

A Note from the Editor

This book was written in a weekend.

It was another crazy idea—bring a group of people together to write an inspirational book about gratitude. In a weekend.

This one topped over 100 contributions, and I'm grateful for each one.

I gave them suggested themes and asked them to keep it to 200 words. (More difficult than it sounds.) They embraced the challenge.

They submitted their pieces within a tight timeline. They proofread their pieces and the ones surrounding theirs.

They cheered with every update and marveled at their own ability.

I am grateful for each and every one of these authors.

Now we share with you the results of that weekend: the inspirational essays, narratives and insights about gratitude for relationships, career, nature, (especially mushrooms) and life. Our intention is this book will empower and uplift you, too, to be a more grateful being.

We've also compiled a list of our favorite causes (found in the back) that support people, pets and even wild birds.

I believe wherever you are right now, whatever you've done to this point, and whatever you intend to create in the future, there is reason to give thanks right now.

Thank you for reading!

My best,

Donna

Donna Kozik

USA Today, *Wall Street Journal* and Amazon bestselling author Creator & Leader, the original Write a Book in a Weekend®

P.S. Want to take part in the next edition of The Community Book Project?

Get on the list to be notified here:
www.CommunityBookProject.com

Contents

Martin Salama

'Tis Better to Give...

"Two kinds of gratitude: The sudden kind we feel for what we take; the larger kind we feel for what we give." ~ Edwin Arlington Robinson

I thought I've always understood and appreciated giving gratitude for what I receive. But, until recently, I don't think I understood gratitude for what I am able to give.

In 2006, there was a bone marrow registry drive for a young girl with leukemia who needed a match. I immediately registered. Unfortunately, no match was found, and she passed away. As the years went by, and life with all of its ups and downs continued, I forgot that I even registered.

Until this year, when I got a call from Gift of Life Marrow Registry: I was a potential match for someone with leukemia. After extensive tests, it was confirmed I was indeed a match to donate stem cells. And I happily did. Now I realize how lucky and grateful I am to be able to possibly save someone's life. So many things could have gone wrong to make it impossible, but they didn't. I was able to donate. It gives me a new understanding of the phrase "'Tis better to give than to receive."

Martin Salama is a life coach and author. In 2013 he published his first book *Recovering from Divorce: 7 Steps to Recover Without Drama to Create a New Life.* You can learn more at www. YourDivorceRecoveryCoach.com.

Holly R. Fitzpatrick

A Reason and Season for Everything

"Each experience will lead you to where you need to be when the time is right." ~ Holly Fitzpatrick

When we acknowledge something as a gift we see the world differently. That different perspective can make the mundane seem like miracles and the tough situations become blessings.

I, like many people, am grateful for my children. See, I was a teen parent and before I was 20 years old I had three healthy babies. While this is not something I recommend, it was not the end of the world for us. A couple years after my last child was born I developed health problems that led to me not being able to have any more children. Had I waited till a more acceptable time to start my family, I would not have been able to.

Being grateful for the timing of everything, even if it might not be the timing you thought was right, will give you peace of mind that there really is a reason and season for everything. Take a moment and look at your past. Find the moments that didn't make sense or did not stand out so much at the time. But, in hindsight, and with the eyes of gratitude you can see the many miracle moments in your life.

Holly Fitzpatrick is the founder of Authentic Self Revealed. As a transformational coach and Hypnotherapist, Holly empowers women to release blocks and barriers while creating the lives they truly desire. Find out more: https://authenticselfrevealedllc.coachesconsole.com.

Dr. Rich Liotta

Gratitude By the Numbers

"Don't count the days, make the days count." ~ Muhammad Ali

Appreciating the beauty I see and feel, my heart glows as I hike along the shore of Lake Champlain on a bright, breezy, and colorful fall day with my wife and Springerdoodle puppy. Even here my mind wanders, this time to the actions I'm taking to heal my cancer, a rare form of multiple myeloma.

Gratitude helps me keep my head in a good place, countering the worries and fears that play in my head. Gratitude is using what life offers to bolster positive thoughts and keep the negative in perspective.

For instance, every month my mind whirls anticipating bloodwork and the numbers that indicate whether the cancer is winning or retreating. For seven months in a row the numbers have offered results to celebrate! My gratitude surges, for the treatment, my supports, and for being pretty healthy despite having cancer. I appreciate all I am doing to beat this. I exercise, eat well, have fun, and use affirmations. Gratitude fuels the fire of healing and empowers attraction.

Truly, every thought counts and every day matters. There are no guarantees, but gratitude illuminates my path with hope. Enjoying each day and relishing what is meaningful is my way to live.

Rich Liotta, Ph.D., is a psychologist, coach, and writer. Find more information and inspiration on his blog or Facebook page, Enrichments for Mind & Spirit. Start here: http://www. changepathsblog.com.

Crystal Rector

The Calling

"Everyone has been made for some particular work, and the desire for that work has been put in every heart."
~ Rumi

Recently I received a text from a client declaring she had just published a review on my animal care services website. She followed up with the message: "You have truly found your calling."

I was not always Crystal the Pet Nanny.

I spent many years doing administrative work in various industries but was increasingly unhappy in those jobs. It became apparent not only to me but to those around me that I was trying—and failing—to fit a square peg into a succession of round holes.

It never occurred to me that I might be able to pay my bills doing exactly what comes naturally until an employer, exasperated with my obvious misery in my customer service position, forced my hand.

Crystal the Pet Nanny was officially born the next day.

That was six years ago.

I don't remember a time when animals didn't bring me joy. Cats, in particular, were an all-consuming passion, so it was effortless for me to learn to understand them. My affection for them came from a deep place: It felt like I was able to connect with them, soul-to-soul.

I have indeed found my calling – my square hole... and I'm grateful for it every day.

Crystal Rector has found her calling caring for animals in the Phoenix Metro area as Crystal the Pet Nanny. Reach her at www. CrystalThePetNanny.com or find her on Facebook.

LaVerne M. Byrd

A Grateful Day

"If you haven't any charity in your heart, you have the worst kind of heart trouble." ~ Bob Hope

Lulu has always expressed concern for the homeless. Even as a young child her heart would break whenever the commercial about hungry children came on the television. So it became natural for her to give money or clothing to charitable organizations. She also volunteered to prepare meals that would be distributed to senior citizens.

Over the years Lulu's employer noticed her efforts to help people in need. The employer decided to set aside a day of "giving back to the community" and appointed her as the leader of the event.

Lulu decided she would adopt a neighborhood school as a charitable outlet. After much planning, the big day arrived for distributing the items. Lulu called a meeting to thank everyone for participating. Because of their compassion, the company was able to supply each student with every item needed to succeed in the classroom.

The overwhelming joy and excitement from the children could not be contained. It became a ripple effect. Everyone was laughing and shedding tears at the same time. That day will no doubt change many lives. It was a lesson for both the receiver and the giver. It was indeed a grateful day!

LaVerne M. Byrd is the creator and leader of the Believe and Succeed Book Club, which is focused on people who have positive influences in the marketplace. Email her at believeandsucceednow@gmail.com.

Katherine Cobb

Living Beyond My Potential

"In our daily lives, we must see that it is not happiness that makes us grateful, but the gratefulness that makes us happy." ~ Albert Clarke

I always knew I was a girl with potential, a girl who was going places. But by the time I turned twenty-five, I was an alcohol- and drug-addicted, jaded-about-love, often unemployable mess.

Luckily for me, twenty-five was my pivotal year.

I met a man and fell in love. Realizing he was worth fighting for, I saw my addiction for what it was, and climbed out of the bottom of my pit and into recovery.

I am eternally grateful for both occurrences. That man became my husband and loved me until I could love myself. He showed me unconditional love and taught me how to give it in return. Conversely, recovery catapulted me into a new stratosphere, one that began a great physical, mental and spiritual metamorphosis that continues to this day.

I no longer have potential—I live it to the fullest every day. I dream, I achieve, I give, I inspire, I love.

Do I count my blessings? You betcha. I give thanks—out loud—to the universe, a higher power, mankind. I thank others. And I share with the world through words spoken and written. My connection to gratitude reminds me that anything is possible, and nothing impossible.

Author Katherine Cobb has published five books, written for several publications in the Mid-Atlantic and won Best Lifestyle Columnist by the WVPA. Find out more at www.katherinecobb. com.

Carol Brusegar

The Transformative Power of Love

"This I know for sure: it is not judgment or isolation that changes us. It is love. Love can transform our negative experiences into new realities. I am so grateful." ~ Carol Brusegar

I had never anticipated standing before groups of inmates in multiple correctional institutions to talk about the power of love. There I was, a silver-haired woman over 70 years of age, disarming them by asking if I reminded them of a grandmother, mother or aunt—or a do-gooder church lady. We all agreed that we make immediate assumptions about people. Then I proceeded to tell my story.

I spoke of years being on "the other side" of the picture as a crime victim multiple times, having friends shot and even killed, and working for the police department. I described how my very first time participating in prison visits with Timothy's Gift Prison Ministry shifted my perspective profoundly. My negative experiences were transformed into a deep passion for this outreach.

The message that people's attitudes can change gives hope to inmates. They express gratitude for that, and for our core messages: 'You are Loved,' 'You Have Great Worth,' 'You are Not Forgotten.' I am profoundly grateful for the transformative power of love available to all of us and for the opportunity to communicate that to people who need it so desperately.

Carol Brusegar is a leading-edge Baby Boomer who is committed to making life after age 50 one of exploration, joy and contribution for herself and others. Her website is http://carolbrusegar.com.

Irena Kay

Gratitude Is a Choice

"Gratitude is a powerful catalyst for happiness. It's the spark that lights a fire of joy in your soul." ~ Amy Collette

Gratitude lets you experience the joy of just being here now. Savor the moment. Let the heart swell with thankfulness for all your blessings.

Imagine your favorite place in nature with all of your senses. See the beauty, hear the sounds of birds or water, feel the sunshine on your skin, smell and even taste the sweet air. Ahhhh…

Instantly your brain will release feel-good hormones, triggered by pathways that were shaped by memories when you felt happy. Feeling grateful, even for little things, gets the same neurotransmitters flowing.

The good news about that? Feeling joyful and happy becomes a choice!

You have the power to control your thoughts and thus your feelings. You know that anything practiced long enough becomes a habit.

"Practice makes perfect", right? Well, not really…Practice only makes permanent; perfect practice makes perfect!

It stands to reason, therefore, to actively practice gratitude. It's such a simple tool; use it!

Pause when you are stressed, look around you, and think about what you can be grateful for right in this moment. Perhaps it's that perfect cup of coffee. Perhaps it's your faithful dog lying at your feet. Choose to be grateful and you choose happiness!

Dr. Irena Kay is a relationship coach, retired physician, and the creator of Married Love Success. She helps people revive the love in their committed relationships. Learn more at https://marriedlovesuccess.com.

Rick Binder

The Sun Will Rise

"You must embrace the darkness before you can see the light." ~ Miyamoto Musashi

I am eternally grateful for the person I've become. After all, it's taken me my entire life to get to this point, and intermingled with the good have been a lot of very dark periods that I've had to overcome. I've survived a great deal of loss and disappointment—material possessions, relationships, financial ruin, career setbacks… The list goes on, but had I not taken the lessons I've learned and overcome I would not be this version of myself.

I am compassionate. I help those in need. I get to walk my daughter down the aisle soon. I get to experience love once more. I place more value on the people in my life than the things in my life. I make the world a better place, and I strive to be an inspiration to others.

None of this would be possible without the setbacks I experienced during those dark days. I am who I am because of who I was, and that's a very good thing. So for those who still suffer, take heart. Tough times pass, and there's an ocean of good times yet to come. Embrace the darkness. Tomorrow the sun will rise.

Rick Binder, author of *The Four Pillars of Cellular Health*, helps others activate their bodies at the cellular level in order to eliminate pain and reduce oxidative stress. http://rickbinder. lifevantage.com.

Rebecca Brown

Rays of Gratitude

"Acknowledging the good that you already have in your life is the foundation for all abundance." ~ Eckhart Tolle

I sit down as I do every evening and open the notebook to a fresh page, a clear canvas.

I draw a circle in the middle and place a heart in the center of the circle.

My practice begins.

As each ray of the sun is drawn I feel a deep sense of gratitude well up from within.

I write about whatever comes to mind – a cup of hot tea, a conversation with my grandmother, a new client, a new connection, the song of a bird outside my window.

Each fills in a ray of the sun as I give thanks for the feeling, the moment, the experience.

This simple exercise allows me to recognize and honor all that I am thankful for this day.

As I draw the final ray and give thanks for the thought written on its line, my heart is full.

I flip through the notebook and see all the sunshine rays of gratitude that fill its pages. I try to pinpoint and describe the feeling within but am at a loss.

It is love. It is joy. It is peace. It is wonder. It is abundance.

It is gratitude.

Rebecca Brown is a Speaker, Coach and Laughter Yoga Teacher based in Reno, NV serving clients globally. Find out more about Rebecca and her work here: www.rebeccabrowncoaching.com.

Patti Smith

Transforming Grief into Gratitude

"The soul would have no rainbow, had the eyes no tears." ~ John Vance Cheney

Was there a sound?

Did the world pause its spinning for just a moment when it happened?

In an instant, she was gone. The mother I had loved so dearly was part of a tangled mess of metal and concrete.

Overwhelming grief consumed me and I took refuge in a tiny hermitage cottage in the country to come to terms with my loss.

No telephone, no computer, no television, no running water. Only an 8 by 12 foot cabin at the tree line, where the snow still clung to the branches of the evergreen forest, and a smallish spider traversing the ceiling to keep me company.

Over three days, I plunged into my grief headfirst and opened my wounded soul to God.

Sobbing subsided as I was shown the truth of what happened, and limiting beliefs I never even knew I had rose up and were released.

I was reborn in that trinity of days. Peace arrived, accompanied by acceptance and wisdom.

I was humbled by the incredible love that surrounded and protected me.

And, finally, the visit of a wolf just before I left. Our eyes locked and I received his blessing, then departed in grace and gratitude.

Patti Smith is a success coach who teaches women CEOs, entrepreneurs and leaders how to create "conscious businesses" for impact and profit. Email her at patti@awesomewealthywoman. com.

Jen DG

Gratitude for Life and Blessings

"When it comes to life the critical thing is whether you take things for granted or take them with gratitude." ~ G. K. Chesterton

Being alive itself is a cause for gratitude.

Have you heard that life is God's gift to us and what we make of ourselves is our gift back to Him?

Even the smallest detail happening in our lives can be a source of gratitude. This can be something that has a price tag such as having a car, house, job or business. It can also be something invaluable such as having good health, peace and support from family and friends.

Nothing should be taken for granted.

When sour thoughts pass by, try to play the game of "finding something good in every situation."

I find gratitude as my antidote to negative emotions. For instance, when I'm feeling down, the first thing I do is to think of the many blessings that I receive each day.

A daily journal helps keep track of these happy memories and a reminder that good things will still come. I like to start my entry with a motivational quote and then list down the things to be thankful for.

Being grateful that we are alive with so much blessing produces happy thoughts. The happy thoughts will then lead to a future full of hope.

Jen DG is an aspiring social entrepreneur who wants to help other like-minded individuals and to give back to the community. Find out more at https://AspiringBusiness.com.

Linda Bittle

The Words Before All Else

"Nature's beauty is a gift that cultivates appreciation and gratitude." ~ Louie Schwartzberg

I was sitting on a damp log next to a fire that had been started with a bow drill the first time I heard the Thanksgiving Address. At 47, I was the oldest "kid" in a class of 18. I'd traveled 1900 miles to an unfamiliar rain forest to learn about nature.

The Thanksgiving Address became a core routine that began each class, community gathering, and even staff meetings at Wilderness Awareness School. Originating with the Iroquois people, it has been shared around the world with instructions to make it personal. It's also called "bringing our minds together."

It begins by giving thanks for people. Next, we express gratitude to the earth, waters, fish, birds and animals. Then trees and plants, the weather, the sun, moon, and stars, then all the things we forgot to mention, and finally, to the Creator.

My faith requires that I give thanks to the Lord for everything. The Thanksgiving Address helps me remember what I am grateful for and gives structure to my prayers.

Adopting the daily practice of expressing gratitude has profoundly changed the way that I view the world. If everyone practiced gratitude, what a force for good we could become!

Linda Bittle lives in rural Idaho with two cats and a small dog. Her blog, This Is Not Where I Thought I Was Going, is found at https://lindabittle.com.

Shona Battersby

Count Your Blessings Daily

"Gratitude is the ability to experience life as a gift. It liberates us from the prison of self-preoccupation." ~ John Ortberg

One way to create peace and joy in your life is to appreciate all the good things, both big and small, that have happened. Take the time to immerse yourself in the emotions and feelings as this will deepen your experience.

It may not always be easy. However, if you create a daily practice of gratitude it will help overcome some of the difficult times in your life.

Here are some ideas to get you started:

Start writing in a gratitude journal. This can be as easy as listing things that you are grateful for. What things happened in your day that put a smile on your face? Music? Children laughing? Mother Nature?

Make sure that you show your appreciation to people in your life and you will notice that this will brighten their day as well as yours. This is one way to spread love and joy to others.

Take photos of things that make you smile. Put them in an album or have them on your mobile phone so that you can look at them and enjoy them.

As you go about your day, remember to find the blessings in as many things as possible.

Shona Battersby does spiritual healing and transformational guidance using reiki, massage, crystals and other tools. Email her at shona.lb@hotmail.com.

Ruth McGarry

Making Lemonade

"When life gives you lemons, give it lemonade." ~ Unknown

Being grateful may not always be easy and I am no exception to this thought. A couple of years ago I was working as an executive for a midsized manufacturing company. I was making good money but I was miserable. I no longer enjoyed what I was doing and dreamed of creating my own business.

The company underwent restructuring and my position was eliminated. I was devastated and thankful at the same time. I wondered where my income would come from, but I was yet excited for a new start. After many months I realized that I was not truly grateful for this event. That didn't surprise me but I knew that was an obstacle for moving forward.

I had many ups and downs over the next 18 months. I knew I needed to look at the good that resulted instead of the pain. By doing so I was able to see how this had helped me to become a better person and find what I was really passionate about: helping others. This wasn't easy. As I now reflect, I am grateful, very grateful, passionately grateful, for this event.

Ruth McGarry is founder and creator of www.createyourhappymonday.com. She offers solutions to help people discover what will make their Monday not a day of dread in their career path.

Uranchimeg (Urna) Belanger

A Child's Gratefulness!

"The roots of all goodness lie in the soil of appreciation for goodness." ~ Dalai Lama

The memories of life awaken me every now and again.

I'm impressed with how my mother taught me life lessons wisely, planting seeds of knowledge. My mother's lessons were mostly given through demonstrations and storytelling, yet sometimes her teaching was done through silence. I truly feel those things I do best in my life come from my mother—given to me as a gift of love.

Parents teach what's important to their children before those children walk into a world that they must connect to on their own. A child gains potential deep within by disciplining himself with self-learning control over his own thoughts and actions.

Children who have gained self-awareness when life throws them out from their comfortable home to the world will live above their potential dreams, mostly unaffected by any life challenges. It will help their flower of life bloom forever.

These learning experiences are achieved while in their youth, the budding period of the flower of life. Life gives the opportunity for every child to go out into the world from their parent's home as they grow up. I'm so grateful, having had a wonderful wise mother, I am still learning now from others in this challenging world.

Urna Belanger is a life coach, freelance author, entrepreneur and parent inspiring all she encounters and connects with. Learn more at: http://www.liveingoodhands.com.

Roberta Gold

Start Your Day with Gratitude

"Gratitude doesn't have to be a serious matter! If you want to thank someone, do it by putting a smile on their face or even making them laugh." ~ Unknown

We have all heard the saying that we should live every day as if it is our last. I am not a fan of this kind of thinking. I suggest we should *live* every day. What I mean by this is we should spend time each day doing something that makes us smile and laugh; spend some time each day being grateful for what we have; spend some time each day doing something for someone else; spend some time each day being mindful of all the beauty around us; and spend some time each day just being silly.

Cultivating mindfulness, gratitude, forgiveness, and kindness has shown to increase our sense of well-being and strengthen our connections with the people who matter most in our lives. In my opinion, gratitude is one of the most moving emotions we have. It gets us out of ourselves and focused on someone or something else.

Studies confirm that people who nurture relationships with fun, laughter, and gratitude, form tighter bonds, report being happier, and live longer. Try starting the day giving thanks for what we have; I believe this will make us happier and more content.

Live every day—with gratitude.

Roberta Gold created "Laughter for the Health of It" and "Laughter Rocks!" with a mission to empower everyone to have a more positive outlook. She's a speaker, author and coach. www.laf4u.com.

Bill McCarthy

Living a Life of Gratitude

"Gratitude is the inward feeling of kindness received. Thankfulness is the natural impulse to express that feeling. Thanksgiving is the following of that impulse." ~ Henry Van Dyke

Gratitude is one of the blessings of life.

The first blessing is life itself, the second is every breath we take, the third is the ability to appreciate our life experiences and the fourth and central blessing is the feeling of gratitude for all the other blessings.

Every morning, at the end of my meditation, I reflect on my experiences and express my gratitude for all the blessings in my life.

I usually find myself in tears as I experience the depth of my gratitude for these blessings.

Beginning each day in this manner sets a tone of appreciation and gratitude for all that I will experience throughout the day.

As the days go on, the depth of my gratitude grows deeper and deeper as my understanding of the preciousness of the gift of life expands.

The source of all life—God, Energy or whatever one chooses to call it—has shown great compassion, by creating us and allowing us the blessing of being alive in this beautiful world.

The only way of expressing my appreciation for this amazing gift is to live in a state of gratitude every day of my life.

Bill McCarthy is a special event, television, and Internet broadcast producer. He is also the founder and president of Unity Foundation. Bill can be reached at unityfoundation1@aol.com.

Kerri McManus

More Flow, Less Hustle

"The goal of life is to make your heartbeat match the beat of the universe, to match your nature with Nature."
~ Joseph Campbell

The grey finch perched on our living room window staring and cheeping at me from the outside, as if to say, "Welcome!" He sat there as if he expected me to open the window and invite him in. And I'll be honest, I nearly did!

After many years of living in a crowded Los Angeles neighborhood and working in an intense office, my husband and I moved to a quiet hillside where we're surrounded by nature. Before we moved, I had tamped down my own nature to navigate the noise in my life. As a sensitive, creative soul, it's no surprise that it manifested in heart palpitations.

Something had to change.

Living and working in this new serene space, I feel as if I've returned to my own natural rhythm. I have a newfound appreciation for my own sensitivity. As I watch the sway of the palm trees in the afternoon wind and the butterflies flitting from one bush to the next, I am creating a natural flow in my own work and I'm able to access my empathic gifts more deeply to help others connect to themselves.

Kerri McManus is a certified life coach who helps artists, entertainment professionals, and creatives connect more deeply to their gifts and talents to consciously create their lives. Find out more at www.kerrimcmanus.com.

Asha Khalil

Grateful to Be

"If ye give thanks, I will give you more." ~ The Koran: Surat Abraham, Verse 7

On Thursday, October 25, 2018, tragedy struck when a group of children and teachers hiking on a school trip near the Dead Sea were swept away by flash floods due to heavy rains. There were fatalities and severe injuries, not only among the children and teachers, but also other people on trips in the area. I cried when I read the news. I was a teacher for 20 years and went on many school trips. It was one of my favorite things to do. I got to visit places I'd never been and got to know my colleagues better. I was able to spend time with the students in a more relaxed environment and have fun with them.

I am so grateful that nothing so horrible happened to my students, colleagues or me on any of those trips. We came close once but, thankfully, it ended with a few minor injuries and perhaps a few scares. Everybody returned home safely.

I pray for those who passed away and those who survived, for they will never be the same.

I feel so much gratitude for being alive and for having those I love with me still. I give thanks every day.

Asha Khalil is an author of children's books, a coach, a teacher, and the creator of SPEAK10 and INK, a creative writing course. To get in touch, go to her Facebook page: www.facebook.com/James.sJourneyBooks.

Judi G. Reid

For Such a Time as This

"And who knows but that you have come to a royal position for such a time as this?" ~ Esther 4:14

Have you ever become angry at what you thought was an injustice? Have you desperately wanted someone to do something about it?

For me, it is the escalation of pornography in our culture and its effects on women and families. I cried out to God, "Why don't You do something?" He replied, "I did. I made you."

In January of 2017, my state legislature faced the opportunity to pass a resolution recognizing pornography as a public health hazard. Many people mocked this concept. Since my lifetime passion has been for the respect and dignity of women, at 73 years old I felt God was choosing me to take the risk and advocate on its behalf.

I had a story. I had the stories of others.

Nervously, I seized the moment to speak before one of the committees.

I prepared my three-minute testimony, determined to be grateful. The committee members had been bombarded with hostility and overloaded with statistics. I wanted to be different.

My first words to them were, "Thank you for the courage to consider passing this legislation."

They listened intently.

My final words were, "I sincerely thank you."

Gratefully, that night it passed.

Judi G. Reid is a #1 Amazon bestselling author and certified Life Breakthrough Coach. She helps women transform their lives, move forward and flourish. Find her at www.WomenOfValue. Org.

Gwyn Goodrow

The Healing Power of Crochet

"Crochet is an accessible art that comes with a license to be prolific." ~ Francine Toukou

A crochet hook and a few colorful scraps of yarn were only the beginning when my mother taught me how to crochet. As a child, I played with crochet patterns and stitches. Yarn transformed into complicated knots of woven fabric. My mother and grandmothers encouraged crafting and lovingly shared technical crochet knowledge.

Our world is often stressful, filled with chaos and uncertainty. That uncertainty manifested after a tumble in my home resulted in bruises, skin abrasions, and a swollen knot on my forehead.

Final diagnosis? Traumatic Brain Injury—and my world exploded.

My mental filing cabinet had dumped its contents. Item by item, I had to relearn physical movement and speech. My brain's dictionary was an untidy clutter of mismatched words and phrases. Crochet skills, deeply ingrained in my memory, however, were graciously available as I fumbled through rehabilitation and regained physical and emotional strength.

With silky soft yarns and familiar stitch patterns, I escaped the rigors of these anxiety-filled circumstances. Skeins of yarn became afghans, scarves, and hats. Inner peace appeared as gradual healing intertwined with crochet. My gratitude for crochet weaves a colorful tale that began with a mother's love, a crochet hook, and some bits of yarn.

Gwyn Goodrow devotes her leisure time to creative yarn hobbies and blogging. She shares her crochet stories and travel adventures on www.crochetgetaway.com.

Joe Raab

Your Super Power

"Only I can change my life. No one can do it for me."
~ Carol Burnett

In my twenties I struggled from intense anxiety—emphasis on intense. I thought a neighbor put a hit out on me. I was actually hit by a cab. I was even hit in the leg by a ricocheting bullet in my neighborhood. The result? I could never relax and always had a tightness in my stomach.

My doctor prescribed medicine, but my anxiety increased. I scheduled an appointment with a psychologist. At the first meeting we just talked. I got nothing except another prescription—and bad side effects. My second appointment was almost an exact duplicate to the first. My dosage increased—and so did the side effects.

Then it hit me: I'm going to have to do this myself. So I decided I would no longer have anxiety. I immediately felt better. And one of my biggest life lessons appeared: choice.

Now I'm not discrediting medicine or the medical field, but I learned I have a choice. I was letting exterior (mostly made-up situations) control me. Nobody was telling me what to do; I was in control.

I chose to be in control, and so can you! We all have the ability to choose how we experience life. It's time.

Joe Raab is a life coach. Through a process of exploration and planning, Joe leads his clients from stuck adults to revolutionary results. Find out more at www.BeDoGetMORE.com.

Veronica Hollingsworth

A Powerful Motivator for Change

"Gratitude turns disappointment into lessons learned, discoveries made, alternatives explored, and new plans set in motion." ~ Auliq-Ice

Perched on the second floor of a shopping complex, a small family resource center is a hub of hope for a rural mountain community. A high-school drop-out saunters through the doors, ashamed of not finishing school, yet determined to attain his GED and get a better job so he can marry his girl. A grandmother raising her grandchild gets help with an overdue bill, and for the first time in her life is taught to budget so she can better provide. A single mother battling addiction acquires a mentor to clean up her life and keep custody of her son.

These people have one thing in common: they came through the door at their lowest point, ready for change. Each one was heard and understood; all had strengths they weren't seeing. The young man had a knack for numbers and is now exploring engineering. The empowered grandmother is teaching her granddaughter smart consumerism. The single mother recognizes her worth, and is setting and meeting goals. They acknowledged their strengths, tapped into gratitude, and used these to carry them forward through challenges.

That's the specialty of this family resource center—focusing on strengths, and using gratitude as fuel for self-motivated change.

Veronica Hollingsworth is a certified health/relationship coach who uses gratitude practices to facilitate real change. Visit her at http://www.veronicahollingsworth.com to learn more.

Nikki Brown

Grateful for My Guide Dogs

"Your vision will become clear only when you can look into your own heart." ~ Carl Jung

In 2004, my life quite literally went to the dogs. My already poor eyesight was getting worse, so I decided to start working with a guide dog. I loved dogs anyway, and I knew a trained guide could help me travel more safely.

This was important since I had two young children to watch out for. In early summer, I met the first of my furry companions and experienced the exhilaration of learning to confidently navigate everything from quiet country roads to the busy streets and subways of New York City without having to worry about tripping over obstacles or stepping into danger. Even then, I had no idea how grateful I would be to have a guide at my side or how much our adventures together would change me.

As my eyesight has gone from bad to worse to totally unusable, my insight has increased exponentially. In many ways, this is because of my amazing guide dogs and the lessons I have learned from them over the years.

Sometimes, when people go blind, they say they have lost their vision. I always say I lost my eyesight, but my vision is actually clearer than it has ever been.

Nikki Brown, The Authors Ally, helps writers find their voice and fuel their confidence. She lives in Texas with her beautiful goofy guide dog, Perry. Connect with her at www.coachnikkib.com/grateful.

Ruben J. Rocha

Welcome to My Heart

"The only way love can last a lifetime is if it is uncon-ditional." ~ Stephen Kendrick

The way my grandmother welcomed me into her home, from childhood through my adult years, continues to influence my life.

She'd stop whatever she was doing, call out my name, throw her arms wide to swallow me up in a tight hug and top it all off with a sweet kiss. It was as if she had been waiting all her life to see me.

She did this with all of her grandkids.

My dad says, "It didn't matter if she hadn't seen you in 24 hours or 24 days. Your reception and welcome were always the same, affectionate and joyful."

There is nothing more important for a child than being welcomed into the home (and heart!) of someone who practices LOVE, unconditionally and exaggeratedly.

An open-armed, open-hearted welcome is a simple, potentially life-changing, experience.

Offer one, and receive one, whenever you can.

Ruben Rocha is an instructor at Diamond Light School of Massage and Healing Arts and has a private massage therapy practice in San Anselmo, Calif. Find him at www.facebook.com/ RJRmassage.

Anne M. Skinner

Messages in the Mess

"Be grateful for what you have right now. Blessings always outnumber failures and difficulties." ~ Unknown

It's easy these days to forget how many blessings we have in our lives. At times I, too, am just as guilty as anyone for letting circumstance cloud over all I have to be grateful for.

Returning today from an awesome week of fun with two of my three granddaughters and two of my three children, I am reminded how during one of the most challenging four-and-a-half years of my life, I have been blessed beyond measure.

I'm so very grateful I've had the opportunity to spend fun, quality time with my children and grand-children: time for self-reflection, healing and time to find myself and my passions again. Amazing how life can change in a flash. As devastating as it may seem, we never know the grander plan that is in play—possibly a wakeup call to remind us of what is truly important, such as all our blessings and who we are destined to be.

So, when life seems difficult, take another look and see what magic is hidden there, and ask "What lesson or course correction might this be?" Trust that you are headed in the right direction and always stop to be grateful for all the wonderful blessings you have!

Anne Skinner: Transformational & Leadership Coach, Mentor, Hypnotist, Trainer and Speaker assists individuals and organizations to tap into their true potential and intentionally grow to achieve their desired success. Email Anne at anneskinner-empowerment@gmail.com.

Susan P. Sloan

Passing It On

"Gratitude is the inward feeling of kindness received. Thankfulness is the natural impulse to express that feeling. Thanksgiving is the following of that impulse." ~ Henry Van Dyke

A stranger approached the table where my family sat in the buffet-style restaurant. We were vacationing with our three children, ages four, eight and nine, and my husband and I had made multiple trips to the buffet bar to assist them in getting their food.

When the stranger approached, I cringed inwardly, afraid that she was going to complain or admonish us for some infraction one of the kids had committed. Instead, she smiled and said, "I just want to congratulate you on having such well-behaved children."

I was so astonished and relieved, I could barely mutter my thanks.

That happened nearly 30 years ago, but it's one of those treasured moments that will stay with me always. Since then I have tried to follow her example. I'm especially sympathetic to parents who struggle with energetic younger children. Any act of kindness is best repaid, I think, by passing it on to others. This is my way of expressing true gratitude to a stranger who made my day.

Susan Sloan is an author who looks for lessons in everyday events. You can see more of her work and contact her at www. silvercurlsblog.wordpress.com.

Daphne Bach Greer

Gratitude: The Secret to Living a Fulfilled Life

"Only when my eyes have adjusted to the dark can I witness the splendor of the moon and stars. Only when I have sat in hopeless loss can I appreciate every blessing." ~ Angela Yuriko Smith

Having gratitude ignites the soul and renews the mind during challenging times, giving us that wholeness and satisfaction that our hearts desire. Gratitude fuels compassion and ignites hope.

Find perspective. Embrace it. Look with eyes of wonder and hope for tomorrow. Take time each day to enjoy the rainbow of colors in that sunset, appreciate being able to hear those birds singing or see the wildlife out your window. Smile with joy when you're able to spend time with family and friends, laughing and adoring such wonderful company.

My point: Among the daily stress, tension, and challenges of life, stop and search for gratitude. We must be cognizant of the incredible gifts we have been bestowed. The miraculous gift it is to even be alive, to experience our five senses, to breathe, to smell, taste, hear and see. To be able to laugh, cry, walk and love.

Gratitude possesses immense life-changing power. If you are willing, it can transform your heart, allowing you to see the world through an eternal perspective and rose-colored glasses.

Intentionally search for that sunshine. Count those blessings. Try to take 15 minutes each day and write down ten things that you are thankful for. You won't be disappointed.

Daphne Bach Greer is the author of *Barely Breathing: Ten Se-crets to Surviving the Loss of a Child and Grief-Diaries: Will We Survive?* **She inspires people to find hope after loss. www. grievinggumdrops.com.**

Fiona-Louise

Gracious Healing

"Gracious words are a honeycomb, sweet to the soul and healing to the bones." ~ Proverbs 16:23-25

I never thought I would be grateful for becoming ill, but I am.

When I first got sick, I was bedridden for six months, exhausted, depleted, and with not much will to go on. My body had crashed and burned, my mind had shutdown, and my soul had ground to a halt.

Then, slowly, but surely, my energy began to return. Step-by-step, day-by-day, I was able to accomplish small things such as having a shower, making a meal and taking a stroll outside. Things that, when I was healthy, I took for granted. Yet, here I was, appreciating every small milestone on the road back to health.

It was a long journey, with twists and turns, setbacks and relapses. I read every self-help book I could get my hands on; delved into counselling, meditation, yoga, reiki—you name it, I tried it!

But the one thing that helped me turn the corner was gratitude. Changing my mindset to thankfulness has given me an inner strength I didn't realize I had. I now see the illness as a blessing because it inspired me to stop and smell the roses.

Gratitude has revealed beauty, love, and kindness. Gratitude has facilitated forgiveness, mended a broken heart, created peace, re-prioritized my life, and enabled healing.

Fiona-Louise is a nutritional therapist, educator and author. Discover her best selling book collaborations and musings here: www.fiona-louise.com.

Grace Kusta Nasralla

Precious Loaves of Bread

"Gratitude makes sense of our past, brings peace for today, and creates a vision for tomorrow." ~ Melody Beattie

It was during the time of the war in Lebanon when one day Mom hollered at me to go and get a pack of bread.

There was a bakery beside us and we had to line up to get it as flour was scarce. I ran down the stairs from our first floor condominium, out the door and down the street where the bakery was to find the line of people extended to the other street block.

In the distance I could hear the sounds of shelling and sniper fire, but we were a family of five and we needed bread for dinner so I had to stay.

As I waited in line I prayed for safety and provision when suddenly I saw a militia car stop and gunmen come out, go into the bakery and start giving out bread randomly, in a rushed manner. They wanted to empty the streets to start a new round of combat. I quickly took my share of bread and fled back home with a grateful heart. Many lives were spared that day.

Gratitude is an attitude that brings joy to the soul even in the middle of strife.

Grace Nasralla is a business instructor and founder of Ontario Small Business Network. Find out more at www.nasralla.net.

Merwyn Evans

Unexpected Perks

"In relation to others, gratitude is good manners; in relation to ourselves, it is a habit of the heart and a spiritual discipline." ~ Daphne Rose Kingma

They never talked about "what-ifs" either between themselves or with me. They were both nonagenarians blessed with good health and able to live independently. Then Dad died.

Mom is always happy to see me. The laughter, kisses and hugs are still the best. She maintains herself independently but, without Dad, she lacks confidence and gets nervous easily. I am now not just her child but also her guide through life's obstacles.

Although I gladly accept this role, it is not necessarily easy. When overwhelmed with the responsibility it brings, I have to take a moment and breathe. Mom is important to me not only for her role in my achievements but for who she is now. One day I won't have her on this earth to cherish. Alleviating her nervousness or doing what she can no longer do physically is a good thing. Being mindful has over time made living my role easier and more joyful.

Unknowingly, Mom has given me several perks: a possible vision of my life in thirty years, the understanding of how I might help my children if they need to care for me, and that my children and I are discussing "what-if's" now!

Merwyn Evans works for a non-profit, is an aspiring writer, loves HEA books (humorous, suspenseful, heartwarming) and enjoys quilting. Merwyn.Evans@gmail.com.

Lisa S. Campbell

Gratitude Brings the Good Stuff

"My day ends and begins with gratitude and joy." ~
Louise Hay

Work hasn't always been easy. I've been laid off in the parking lot, punished with writing an essay about "difficult conversations" (did well on that one), and fired more than once. I've lived check-to-check and on even less.

Despite the challenges, I'm scrappy, I bounce back quickly and mostly, I'm grateful.

Gratitude. The most magical word in all of the languages. How do I know? Just try being complain-y and entitled while being grateful at the same time. You'll find you just can't! So might as well pick gratitude. There are techniques, though.

The magic bullet when I'm feeling down about work or prosperity is to write a gratitude list. I pull out a napkin, scrap of paper, whatever is near, and just start listing. It puts me in a frame of mind that inspires and motivates, while helping me to attract more of the good stuff.

These scraps of paper go in a box along with a few dollars. I intend to spend the money at the end of the year on something I would love to have. And then, I'll count my blessings on those scraps of paper and begin filling the box again.

Lisa Campbell is a native Californian, business consultant, college professor and copywriter. Reach her at lscgeemail@ gmail.com.

Dr. Ola B. Madsen

The Secret Unlocked

"If you want to live an extraordinary life, you have to give up the things that are part of an ordinary life."~ Srinivas Rao

Ever noticed that when you are feeling crappy, the whole world seems crappy and unfair? But when you are in a good mood, the whole world appears friendly and wonderful and nothing can bring you down. Key thought: The world is no different on those days. You are different.

Earl Nightingale had a program called "The Strangest Secret" and he said, "You become what you think about most of the time." The idea is, we can attract anything we want into our lives by seeing in our mind's eye the desired results, expecting good things to happen, being grateful, showing appreciation and taking action. How you think in any moment determines how you feel and act in any situation.

Create a gratitude journal and every day write three things you are grateful for. Gratitude unlocks our positive view of the world. We can see how good things really are and then our mind is opened up to so many possibilities. The world does not change; you change. It's up to you. This is the real and awesome secret of a gratitude journal. Start one now and experience abundance, contentment, happiness, and peace like never before.

Dr. Ola B. Madsen is a motivational speaker and health and wellness coach. Get his free Weekly Empowering Thought at www.olamadsen.com.

Carol Trant Dean

The Best Gift

"Every good gift and every perfect gift comes from above." ~ James 1:17

Nine years ago, right before Christmas, I was driving home from my office when I received a call from my daughter. At that time she and her husband lived about eight hours away. Initially, we discussed our day's activities, but I could tell she was rather excited by the tone of her voice.

She then revealed the purpose of her call: she had been to the doctor that day and discovered that she was pregnant with our first grandchild! I was so excited I wanted to shout, but because I was retrieving the mail, I decided against it. We ended our call all too soon with her promising to let me know how she was feeling, when her doctor's appointments were scheduled, the sex of the baby, what colors she wanted to use in the nursery, prospective names for the baby; in summary, everything.

After all, this was to be our very first grandchild and I was over the moon in love already. We have five beautiful grandchildren now that we love dearly, but I'll never forget how thankful we were for our first.

Carol Trant Dean resides in Alabama with her husband and old rescue dog where she enjoys missions, foreign travel, and especially spending time with her grandchildren.

Connie Ragen Green

Grateful for Every Day

"Whatever our individual troubles and challenges may be, it's important to pause every now and then to appreciate all that we have, on every level." ~ Shakti Gawain

Every morning when I awake and my feet touch the floor I express my gratitude for being alive. I thank God for everything I am and all that I have and for everything that is possible during this magnificent day.

But I didn't always feel this way.

I was a complainer for most of my life, living an existence of mediocrity, going through the motions, blaming others for what I did not have and could not do. I played the victim, unable to achieve even the smallest goals because of so many issues I refused to call my own.

Then one day I decided to take full responsibility for everything, big and small that occurred in my life. For the first time since childhood, I exhaled. Breathing out the sadness, the loneliness, and the goals not achieved.

And when I had let it all out, I took a long, steady, focused breath in. In with the new, the possible, and the dreams. My gratitude grows with each new day. I have the power to create the life I choose. It's up to me as to what I will manifest. Sometimes I even surprise myself with what I come up with.

Connie Ragen Green is an author and online marketing strategist who works with entrepreneurs on six continents. Find out more at https://ConnieRagenGreen.com.

Heidi Miller-Ford

Happy as You Are

"Have gratitude for all that you have, and you can be happy exactly as you are." ~ Mandy Ingber

I believe true gratitude comes from being content in whatever state we are in and focusing on what really matters. You can find it in the most unexpected ways.

It can be your husband losing his job, but appreciating the fact that he gets to spend more time with the family. Or perhaps being worn out from all the noise and chaos of raising children, only to remember they won't be around forever and the house will be strangely quiet one day. It could be dealing with a huge mess in the kitchen while your children are helping cook, but realizing you are making precious memories for years down the road.

It's hard to find gratitude in these situations when looking at them from the wrong angle. There will always be those who have it better than you, but I guarantee you there are also those who have it far worse. So, take a good look at your life and all that you have. There you will find the gift of gratitude in being happy exactly as you are.

Heidi's a wife and homeschool mom of three who runs a blog helping homeschool families find ways to make their busy, demanding, but fulfilling lifestyles easier. She can be found at https://theunexpectedhomeschooler.com.

Marcelle della Faille

Let's Create Peace in Our World

"Gratitude can transform common days into thanksgivings, turn routine jobs into joy, and change ordinary opportunities into blessings." ~ William Arthur Ward

When I feel down and a bit depressed—yes, it happens, even to an expert in universal laws—I focus even more on the tasks that bring me joy: writing, sharing, playing with the Universal Magic in practical situations.

I cannot spend a day without "doing" this and being in that frequency. And because I chose to teach this concept as my business, and as I decided recently to attune my desires to new values,

I feel so blessed by my lifestyle: a great family, a magnificent business community, a beautiful environment, new opportunities and new beginnings.

What I love the most in my work is creating new games with the Universe, expressing gratitude being the primary one.

Each day, I intend to express gratefulness from the minute I'm awake to the minute I fall asleep. And having a community of people listening to my teachings and reading my books helps me to feel grateful for the contribution I'm making to the world. This helps me feel at one with each of my fellow people and at peace with the world.

Let's create peace in our own world today: just be grateful for what is—for you and all of us.

Marcelle della Faille is a writer and trainer of financial abundance coaches, helping them develop their love and passion into a profitable and fulfilling business. Find out more at https://loveandmoneyalchemy.com/free-chapter-make-peace-with-money/.

Carol Stockall

Glitter with Gratitude

"Sprinkle the world with gratitude and it sparkles with happiness." ~ Carol Stockall, MD

Like the glitter of fairy dust, gratitude has powerful magic more precious than gold. Gratitude makes eyes twinkle with appreciation and hearts glow with happiness. A simple thank you can take a frown and turn it upside-down.

When you show appreciation you can see it smiling right back at you. It's like a hug because when you give one, you get one right back. Who isn't grateful for a thank you?

The magic of gratitude is a gift that must be opened and shared to be experienced and enjoyed. Tossing out thanks like confetti creates contagious feelings of celebration. Never miss an opportunity to give thanks. Never take a thank you for granted. Public and private displays of gratitude bring intimacy and intensity to your relationships.

Gratitude is also a gift you give yourself. Counting your blessings is a healing salve for a weary soul. An attitude of gratitude creates a paradigm shift that can turn your burdens into blessings and your sadness into gladness.

Let gratitude spark your joy. Make counting your blessings and sharing your gratitude with others a daily habit. Begin and end each day sprinkling "thank yous" and watch your world sparkle with happiness.

Carol Stockall, M.D., is a physician, coach and counselor who inspires people to build resilience and flourish. Find out more at www.carolstockall.com.

Michelle Francik

I Am So Grateful!

"We often take for granted the very things that most deserve our gratitude." ~ Cynthia Ozick

I'm grateful for the multitude of scars across my belly because they show that I am a survivor. They show that my life has not been easy. They show that I know how to heal.

I'm grateful for my two sons. Each of them is a joy, a source of pride, and a pain in the butt: just like their mama. One is friendly, talkative, anxious and wants to be the center of attention. One is quiet, reflective, laid back and serious. But they are both good men; and they know how to love and to be respectful. Even If I have done nothing else right in my life, I have raised two fine men.

I'm grateful for my son's cat, Oreo. Even though he likes to jump onto my bed and roll into my face, waking me up and making me sneeze, he loves me even when I'm cranky. Even when I'm sick.

I'm grateful for being alive. The pain is incredible, the fear is immobilizing. But every morning the sun comes up. Every morning I have another opportunity to make today the very best day of my life. And I'm grateful that I'm being given that opportunity.

Michelle Francik is a writer and a ghostwriter. You can find her on Upwork and email her at: mfrancik.author@gmail.com.

Michelle Barrial

Health Is Wealth

"The greatest wealth is health." ~ Virgil

I am most grateful for my health and my life since I have had my share of health crises. I almost didn't make it to being alive at birth since I had the umbilical cord wrapped around my body. My mother said the doctors called for emergency back up as a code blue.

When I was less than a year I almost died from pneumonia and had to be hospitalized for a week in intensive care. Many years later, I noticed I was dropping weight due to hemorrhaging during my menstrual cycle, which was increasingly painful and I had severe anemia.

My doctor told me I had to have a hysterectomy to remove two large fibroids from my uterus. I was worried and scared since I hadn't had surgery before.

But, after I recovered from the surgery, I felt like I received quality of life back since I had no pain, no more shortness of breath and I could run and walk again. I feel blessed and have transformed my life through yoga and dietary changes.

I know that having good health is wealth!

Michelle Barrial is a life transformation coach who specializes in helping people through difficult life changes to get clarity and feel peace of mind. She can be reached at: michelle@healingheartsandminds.com.

Mary Anne Strange

A Daily Gift in 'Thank You'

"A heartfelt 'thank you' are two of the most powerful words we can say." ~ Mary Anne Strange

In my family, opening presents has always been a special ceremony. Presents are wrapped and opened with care, appreciation and gratitude. I love giving presents and to this day it is a way of making someone feel both special and valued. Yet I benefit too as there is pleasure in the giving.

Physical gifts work well when spaced over time or for special occasions. The gift of gratitude can be present daily through the spoken word. Many of us were trained as children to say "thank you." It was, though, as an adult that I discovered the power of those words.

In today's busy world, people appreciate it when you pause to acknowledge their efforts. A sincere "thank you" is simple and efficient. Expand the "thank you" with some detail to increase the direct appreciation and impact.

The other day, my husband was driving me to the station. We were in a rush. Stress was in the air. I paused and said, "Thank you for going to such trouble to help me catch the train." My husband beamed and we both felt calmer.

And that is the secret of gratitude and the words "thank you." The recipient feels valued and acknowledged. But gratitude also makes the speaker feel happier, more present and connected.

Mary Anne Strange helps entrepreneurs master the art of sharing their message and becoming more visible through live and virtual public speaking. Find out more at www.Speakto-Engage.com.

Paula S Webb

Be Thankful, Show Gratitude

"Thankfulness is the beginning of gratitude. Gratitude is the completion of thankfulness. Thankfulness may consist merely of words. Gratitude is shown in acts." ~ Henri Frederic Amiel

I am often blessed by the kindness of others. So it stands to reason, that I'd want to return the favor. While there are many ways to show appreciation to others, try matching the gift with the original kindness. If someone pays for lunch, invite them out the next week and pay for their lunch. At the very least, remember to say "thank you." Mention the act itself and the person's name and it becomes personalized. You can also send a thank you card, letter, email, or call them.

There are many ways to acknowledge the kindness of others. You can cook a meal, gift them their favorite coffee, wine, snack, or fragrance. You could also offer to clean someone's house, yard, or babysit, freeing up their time to help others. Did someone allow you to crash on their couch? Make sure you're a good house guest, and say thank you by offering to buy donuts, make breakfast or wash the breakfast dishes. Did someone loan you their car? Repay them by returning it with a full tank of gas. Has someone done a kindness for you recently? How will you show your gratitude?

Paula lives in east Texas and loves writing, nature, and trying new things. You can learn more about Paula and her adventures by visiting www.paulawebbhome.com.

Norma Bonner Elmore

The Perfect Renter

"Gratitude is an art of painting an adversity into a lovely picture." ~ Kak Sri

Last year, cleaning out my vacation house on Lookout Mountain was the farthest thing from my mind. But my friend became the chairman of a committee to find a parsonage on the mountain for their new pastor. She knew my house was vacant and asked if I would consider renting it.

I had to make a decision. The house was packed full of family treasures. We could not move everything to our farmhouse because it was full of inherited treasures.

After considerable thought, I decided to move the objects that I could not live without to the farmhouse, let my children have anything they wanted, and then donate the rest to the church. The congregation loved the idea and they pitched in to get the house cleaned out.

Now, a year later, I owe a gift of gratitude to my friend. My perfect renters left the house in great shape and I was able to put it on the market the day they moved out. My real estate agent said that the room colors they painted the walls and the wood flooring they had installed were exactly what buyers were currently looking for in a home.

Thank you, Elaine Hefner and Parkview Community Church.

Norma Bonner Elmore, Ed.D., is a singer and specialist in music styles. Her email address is norma.elmore@yahoo.com.

Linda Faulk

Be Grateful for Every Day

"Embrace every new day with gratitude, hope, and love." ~ Lailah Gifty Akita

You are not the same person that you were yesterday. Whatever happened yesterday is finished. You may have been wronged, you may have been hurt or you may have hurt someone else. But today you have a fresh start. Even on good days, I am grateful for another fresh start. I learned this lesson of daily gratitude long ago, but still practice it today.

When my husband died many years ago, I thought it was the end of my life as well. I could not see past my own pain. Then I got a health scare myself. I prayed for another day and vowed that I would embrace each day I was granted. I gave thanks for the next day, and every day since. Just a simple step of being grateful brought me from depression and gave me the courage to begin again. Thirty years later, I am still grateful.

All life's blessings begin with gratitude. Spend a few minutes each morning to jot down all the things you are grateful for and your day will improve. Use a few minutes each night to do the same and you will sleep better. And with each new day, give thanks.

Linda Faulk is a high school math teacher, writer, and entrepreneur. You can contact her at mucholderandbetter@gmail.com.

Leasha West

Ritualize a Life of Gratitude

"Gratitude is one of life's remarkable shortcuts to happiness." ~ Barry Neil Kaufman

Remember when you were a kid and adults always taught you to say thank you? Somehow, when we grow up, saying thank you tends to subside; and with some, is eliminated altogether. I believe this is not due to a shortage of things to be thankful for but rather a lack of mindfulness.

To cultivate a mindfulness of gratitude, I have two surefire rituals to bring appreciation to the forefront of your life.

First, start a gratitude journal. Every night before bed, record 10 things you are thankful for. Coming up with 10 things daily forces you to give thought and closely evaluate your life. Keep the journal by your bed and habitually do this every night. As you incorporate this ritual, each day you will become aware of more things you are grateful for.

Next, send a minimum of two handwritten thank you or congratulatory notes each week. This ritual will cause you to look for opportunities to write your sentiments of gratitude and celebrate another person's win. Receiving a handwritten note in this digital age is special and memorable.

These two powerful rituals will improve satisfaction with your life.

And don't forget to say thank you.

Leasha West is the CEO of West Financial Group, decorated Marine Corps Veteran, member of Million Dollar Round Table and Forbes Finance Council. Connect with her at leasha@west-financialgroup.com.

Maxiann Forbes

Gratitude Can Improve Our Relationships

"Give, and it will be given to you!" ~ Luke 6:38

Have you ever given someone a gift and they didn't say, "thank you?"

This happened to me recently and got me thinking: should I be upset that they didn't express their gratitude for receiving my gift? Although I didn't expect to be physically given something in return, a thank you would have been appreciated. When we show our sincere gratitude, we make the giver feel valued.

The gift can be something lavish or something simple such as a kind word or practical help. Reciprocating to anyone that does a kind deed for us can help improve our relationship with them. Whether the person is our boss, friend, neighbor, relative or spouse, we should remember to always be thankful.

If expressing gratitude does not come naturally to you, practice giving. Look for small ways to show gratitude towards others. You can also look for opportunities to show others gratitude.

When we are genuinely appreciative, it encourages people to extend thanksgiving to us. However, our motivation for giving gifts should never be to receive one in return. Always remember that no matter how big or small the gift we receive, we should show our appreciation for their thoughtfulness and effort.

Maxiann Forbes is a faith-based blogger and owner of the website, Scriptural Gems. You can read more of her work at https:// scripturalgems.com.

Shari-Jayne Boda

The Blessings That Gratitude Brings

"Gratitude makes sense of our past, brings peace for today and creates a vision for tomorrow." ~ Melody Beattie

Martha was always a cup half empty kind of girl. She was raised in a strict household where children were to be seen and not heard, to make do and mend and never to ask for anything. Her life was always a struggle, but Martha grimly soldiered on.

She married in her thirties and two years later, just a week before Christmas, Martha's 40-year-old husband suffered a fatal heart attack.

Her neighbors rallied round, offering help and financial assistance with the funeral expenses, but Martha, true to her upbringing, declined, as she refused to accept what she viewed as charity. One day a neighbor spotted Martha leaving the local store and struck up a conversation as she walked beside her. Martha looked frail and a shadow of her former self.

Her neighbor smiled warmly and explained what a wonderful gift she would be giving to her community by allowing them to help her. Martha looked confused, but her neighbor explained, "Be thankful and welcome the help you're offered because you will be granting others the pleasure that giving brings."

By doing so, Martha's world and the lives of those around her transformed thanks to the blessings that receiving with gratitude brings.

Shari-Jayne Boda is an International Spiritual Life and Prosperity Coach, Hypnotherapist and Counsellor who guides people to live authentically and in tune with their higher self. Email her at contact@mindalchemy.co.uk.

Ellen Watts

A Deep Dive into Gratitude

"Sometimes, what we need the most, is some quiet space and a new perspective." ~ Ellen Watts

I sit, staring into my coffee, feeling unsupported, let-down, weary.

I decide to change because this pity party is a thought, and a thought can be changed. So I begin my descent into gratitude, starting with what's right in front of me. "I'm grateful for this coffee; grateful to the server who brought it to me and the barista who made it for me."

I dive deeper still. "I'm grateful to the person who first discovered coffee and that roasting and grinding it makes it taste so good. I'm thankful that I wasn't the one who had to grow this coffee plant, tend it, protect it, harvest it."

I visualize all the people, working long hours in many conditions to roast it, sort it, bag it, pack it in huge containers and drive it to the docks. The pilot who flew the plane, the attendants, the drivers who transported it to the stores, the café owner who bought the coffee and trained her staff. And I realize just how many people have served me, to bring me this one cup of coffee and allow me this moment of rest. "Thank you all."

I feel deeply supported, up-lifted and inspired.

Ellen Watts is the award winning author of *Cosmic Ordering Made Easier - How to Get More of What You Want, More Often* and the founder of The Co-Creator's Club www.be-unlimited-with-ellen-watts.com.

Diana Bianchi

Sam

"A dog is the only creature in the world that loves you more than himself!" ~ Josh Billings

1, 2, 3, 4... I slowly inhale and then count again until four while keeping the air in my lungs and then exhale counting to eight. I do it two more times, eyes closed.

Next stage: I'm setting my focus on my heart area and I'm calling the image of my cute, small furry ball of love, Sam. As soon as I picture him, sleeping all curled up or joyfully playing around me, my heart has widely opened and sent waves of energy at miles around. I'm ready now to connect to the Akashic record field.

I was using heart-opening techniques from the moment I was taught Reiki, years before, but it never felt so easy to be in the state of gratitude as it is now, picturing my dog, or, I might say, becoming aware of the waves of love he's always sending me.

I'm literally melting each and every time this is happening and this state of pure love he's bringing me into is the best gift I could ever receive and I'll be forever grateful to him for this.

Diana Bianchi is an intuitive business coach helping entrepreneurs create their successful business as a playground of self-expression, using Akashic Records readings. Find out more at https://www.facebook.com/DianaBianchiCoach/.

Lorrie M. Nixon

Meeting Mary

"Wear gratitude like a cloak and it will feed every corner of your life." ~ Rumi

My senior mother and I went to deliver donated food to an elderly woman, Mary, who doesn't go out. We needed help locating her apartment, but finally did and began carrying in the food.

Mary was amazed. She hugged me, her whole body shaking as she cried, "Is this food really for me?" As my mother brought in fresh fruit and chicken, Mary sagged in gratitude, murmuring "Thank you, Lord," tears streaming down her cheeks.

She was suffering and seemed overwhelmed to find that someone cared. We had tears in our eyes too as Mary held us close. Looking at her, you would not know the difficulties she was enduring. Neighbors waved as she stood on the porch, Mary happily waving back.

Organizers told us later that we had gone to the wrong apartment. "No," I insisted, "meeting Mary was no mistake. We had arrived exactly where we needed to be."

The gift of gratitude in this story is mine, though. I won't forget the 88-year-old woman's tears of relief as they spilled from her cheeks to mine. I felt a part of what this world can be when we take the time and make the effort.

Lorrie Nixon is a global consultant with clients in the USA, Greece, Italy, Poland and Denmark. She is a #1 bestselling author on Amazon. Learn more at https://www.linkedin.com/in/lorrienixon/.

Charlisa E. Delancy-Cash

My Favorite Seasons

"It is in the quieted crucible of your personal, private suffering that your noblest dreams are born and God's greatest gifts are given." ~ Wintley Phipps

The date November 4, 2014, is etched in my mind. It was the day that my husband confessed to having yet another affair, and I asked him to leave.

Four years have passed since then. I now reflect on when I was going through after the initial shock of it all. At the time, the pain and agony were so fierce that I did not know how I was going to pick up the pieces.

But life's seasons change. Winter melts into spring. Spring leaps into summer. Summer unwinds into fall. The seasons brought change for me, too. After separating from my husband, I met a man the following year, and, with him, I had a wonderful summer and a beautiful autumn.

I do not dwell on the winters of my life anymore. Instead I find joy in the warm seasons of summer and autumn. I am mindful to make wonderful memories in these, my happy seasons.

Summer and autumn are my two favorite seasons, as they are God's two gifts to me. They are also the names of my two precious daughters who are now one year and two years old respectively.

Charlisa E. Delancy-Cash is a divorced mother of two who enjoys getting her feet wet in the Bahamas. Her Facebook link is https://www.facebook.com/charlisac.

Carol Caffey

Gratitude Works!

"In everything give thanks." ~ St. Paul the Apostle

What? Give thanks in absolutely everything? It turns out that is excellent advice. Scientific studies show being grateful is a way to increase happiness and satisfaction with your life. Studies also indicate gratitude benefits your physical health in dozens of ways.

Expressing your gratitude to the people around you in tangible ways even increases the rewards. One of them is that your relationships will be more fulfilling. Loving ties will be strengthened. People will want to be around this genuinely positive energy.

It is also especially rewarding to list things you are grateful for every day. It doesn't even have to be on paper. Reminding yourself often during the day of whatever you are grateful for is a powerfully good habit to cultivate.

It seems to be a truism that whatever we focus on increases. It helps in the going to sleep process to think about things that happened during the day that you are grateful for. It is an effective tool for getting to sleep and a way to program yourself for good things to happen tomorrow.

Thankfulness reaps a bountiful harvest, and the fields are always ready to be harvested.

Carol Caffey is an avid student of how to live better on the planet. Email her at thefield000@gmail.com.

Barbara Watson

Gratitude Renewed

"Gratitude turns what we have into enough." ~ Unknown

Change your life; change the world! An attitude of gratitude can truly help you do that. How? Feeling grateful for all the good people and all the good things in your life, something you can do on a daily basis, helps you move into the spiritual dimension of life. Bringing those you value into your awareness helps you move more smoothly into that space beyond the mind where miracles lie, just waiting for you to find them.

How can you begin? Grab a little book of some kind and write down three people or things that you are grateful for. Do the same thing the next day and then every day thereafter. You will be adding three more items to your list each day, renewing your attitude of gratitude as you go.

After one month of doing this, you will have almost 100 items on your gratitude list. Imagine how long that list would be after one year!

What are you waiting for? There's no time like the present. Grab a pen and paper and begin your list right now!

Barbara Watson, a retired registered nurse and holistic wellness educator, tracks emerging trends in stress management and meditation to help her students stay a step ahead. Learn more at www.barbarawatson.ca.

Nancy J. Haberstich

A Full Circle of Gratitude

"Gratitude turns what we have into enough." ~ Unknown

It was Thanksgiving Day in Liberia. Doris, Jerry and I set out on a two-mile hike through the rubber forest to a leper colony. The residents are elderly, no longer infectious but still ostracized.

I visited a man who was blind with no hands and only a portion of a foot on his one skinny leg. He scooted across the concrete floor of his mud-brick dwelling to welcome me. With no hand to shake, and no vision to see the smile I brought him, he still thanked me repeatedly for coming. Doris says that worse than the physical impairments is the pain of feeling forgotten. We learned that their water pump was broken and the closest water source was nearly a mile away. Jerry was able to fix the pump with the wrench he always carried in his back pocket. The water began flowing, along with the gratitude.

As we walked back home, I was overwhelmed with gratitude for my shoes, the feet I had to fill them and good health that enabled me to hike four miles in an afternoon. That day we experienced a full circle of gratitude. For that precious memory, I will always be grateful.

Nancy Haberstich, RN is the founder of Nanobugs, Inc. She provides STEM resource materials to help people of all ages learn practical microbiology and infection prevention. Learn more at www.nanobugs.com.

Mary Duggan

Breaths That Open Your Heart

"Gratitude is the memory of the heart." ~ Jean Baptiste Massieu

The body is hard-wired for self-preservation. Alert to threats and dangers, it doesn't distinguish between the physical and the psychological.

Fear, anger, and shame penetrate the heart at lightning speed, but the softer, warmer feelings take longer to find a way in. They don't break the door down; they wait to be invited.

This happens to gratitude. We give it a glance of recognition and go back to scanning the horizon for danger. Gratitude never even gets across the threshold, let alone into our hearts.

Try this powerful way of enhancing your gratitude practice. It's a beautiful thing to do at the start and end of the day. Let yourself be aware of things that you are grateful for. Write them down.

Look at what you've written, say each one out loud and give your attention to the physical feeling of gratitude. What kind of sensation is it? Where is it located?

Take three deep, slow breaths as you let gratitude enter and fill your heart. You might want to gently place your hands over your heart as you do this. Feel your heart expand. Embrace gratitude and carry it with you always.

Mary Duggan shows people how to tap into their creativity for personal and professional growth. Find out more at www. cockleshellcreative.com.

Rachel A. Kowalski

The Best, Worst Thing

"Life is a series of thousands of tiny miracles. Notice them." ~ Unknown

Neil Young was softly singing in the background, "There's a full moon rising, let's go dancing in the light…I want to see you dance again…on this Harvest Moon," as my mom and I lightly two-stepped around her hospital room.

She had recently undergone surgery to remove a brain tumor, which thankfully turned out to be non-malignant. Her doctors encouraged our dance sessions, as they not only lifted her spirits, but also aided in the reconnection of her brain synapses.

Thinking back to those days of her recovery, I can still see her smiling face, her head wrapped in bandages, and hear her sweet, contagious giggle-laugh as we twirled around the room.

Prior to my mom's brain tumor, I was moodier and had a sharper temper. After spending five-plus months in the hospital and during recovery with my mom, I now have a different lens on life. Are those who I love and care about alive and kicking? Yes? Then anything else is manageable. I've learned to take life in stride and enjoy every moment.

This is why my mom's brain tumor was the best, worst thing that ever happened to me, and I am forever grateful for the experience. Not to mention, she is alive and well today!

Rachel A. Kowalski is an attorney, ghostwriter and creative force behind Free Wave Productions, Inc. Find out more about Rachel at https://www.linkedin.com/in/rachelkowalski/.

Joel Bloom

Thankful for a Stitch

"Enjoy the little things, for one day you may look back and realize they were the big things." ~ Robert Brault

Don't you just LOVE to laugh? It can be so wonderfully contagious, ease away tension, and even exercise your abs!

I am so grateful for the role of laughter in my life. Some of my favorite memories of my departed brother and parents have everything to do with being brought closer together and laughing at a joke or a TV show. Now, older with my own family, laughter is just as present.

My wife has been known to literally laugh so hard she gets a stitch in her side and my daughter will often laugh so hard she cries! I am so thankful we are all actively overcoming our "negativity bias," something scientists say we humans have evolved with, where we are pre-disposed to more prominently feel negative emotions like stress and fear. Doesn't calm and positive sound so much better?

Kids don't have to make a conscious effort to laugh like adults... they laugh naturally and far more often than adults, according to studies. Thankfully Siri and Alexa can now tell us jokes, so there is truly no excuse not to help yourself and others laugh all the way to feeling happier and healthier every day!

Joel Bloom is a loving father and husband whose life long goals include helping others to move in a positive direction in their lives. Email him at giftofgratitude@yahoo.com.

Carla Parvin

The Wonderful Lure of Mushrooms

"Everybody needs beauty...places to play in and pray in where nature may heal and cheer and give strength to the body and soul alike." ~ John Muir

For me, that place has always been the woods. I am grateful for every chance to be in the woods because that is where I find mushrooms—tasty, healthy, soul-saving mushrooms.

Mushrooms are tasty (think Chanterelles in cream sauce) and a great source of healthy non-meat protein. My husband shares my love of mushrooms—they lure us out of the house and into the woods, and I am grateful for that.

We grew up playing in the woods, spending every possible moment outside. But as we became adults, the woods became an ever-smaller part of life as raising a family consumed our time. In our sixties, arthritis came calling and the woods retreated even further from our lives.

Then I discovered mushrooms. I learned how to find and identify them, how to cook them, how to grow them—I was hooked. My husband started going with me. We explored acres of woods on an ATV, and we were in heaven. The ATV gave us legs—four-wheel drive legs, no less!

After a few productive trips where Chanterelles, Lion's Mane and Black Trumpets were found (resulting in delightful feasts), he too was hooked.

Our mantra has become: "Mushrooms are calling, and we must go."

Carla Parvin (wife and mother of three with two grandchildren) is a writer and operations manager of *WNC Woman* **magazine. You can find her musings on mushrooms and other topics at www. journeywithnature.com.**

LC Plaunt

Find the Joy

"Can I see the things to be grateful for? If I can see the things to be grateful for, I can find joy." ~ Ann Voskamp

There is always something to be thankful for. You may say, "But you don't know what I'm going through!" It's true, I don't, but I do know we all have tough stuff. I know it can be hard to be thankful in those situations. We tend to focus on the problem, and what we don't have. I find when I focus on what I do have instead, I am much more optimistic and better able to face the challenges.

Even the tough stuff can be a blessing in disguise. It may make us stronger, teach us a valuable lesson, or motivate us to do something great. It is amazing the number of charitable organizations that have been born out of illness or grief. Sometimes you are given a gift that you wouldn't have had if the difficult circumstances hadn't happened—like a stronger relationship with friends and family, or a new career direction that is better than the one before. So take a look at your situation. What can you learn? How can you turn your situation around? Focus on the positive, and you will find the joy.

LC Plaunt is an educator, copyeditor, and writer. She loves to teach people about language and has taught students from elementary to the post-graduate level. Find her at https://www.plaunt.com.

Steve Sponseller

Four Powerful Paws

"A dog is the only thing on earth that loves you more than he loves himself." ~ Josh Billings

Four paws left a permanent impression on my heart! I'm grateful that I had an opportunity to spend almost 16 years with Harley, a Yellow Labrador Retriever who was an important part of our family.

Harley had a unique personality and always seemed to know what I was thinking. On many occasions when I was deep in thought, I would notice him sitting quietly and looking at me. As soon as he saw me look up, he came over to visit me—always wagging his tail.

He knew I was busy, but also understood it was time to say "Hi" when my critical thinking was done.

Harley was a master at communicating through his body language. Wagging his tail, turning his head sideways, or running in circles. He knew what I was feeling and just wanted to help me by being nearby. If I was sad, he would jump around and act silly. If I was stressed, he would just stand next to me until I started petting him—a fantastic stress reliever!

I'm grateful for the years I spent with Harley and appreciate the many lessons he taught me about communicating and interacting with others.

Steve Sponseller is an intellectual property attorney who helps entrepreneurs and business leaders identify and protect their innovative ideas. Find out more at www.SteveSponseller.com.

Diane Kurzava

Choose Gratitude in Every Situation

"Start your children off on the way they should go, and even when they are old they will not turn from it." ~ Proverbs 22:6

My granddaughter had the amazing opportunity to participate in a huge high school marching band competition. Huge being 74 bands from 15 states. After a fantastic performance in the preliminaries, their band was one of only 14 to proceed to the finals.

The following day, after another great performance, they learned they placed thirteenth. A big victory since 60 of the bands didn't even make it to the finals. However, many parents spoke of their disappointment in the results. After all, the band frequently placed first, second or third. While this was not the outcome many expected, gratitude had the opportunity to shine!

Gratitude the kids were able to participate. Gratitude the buses carrying them on this four-hour journey were well maintained and safe. Gratitude they outmarched and outplayed 61 other bands to achieve a thirteenth place ranking while other teams headed home.

It's up to us as parents and grandparents to let the gratitude, and not the disappointment, shine through and carry us home and into the next competition. Gratitude is in the attitude. Start them off right on the way it works.

Diane Kurzava runs a daycare, which includes her grandchildren, and owns a business specializing in natural products and education for health, wellness, home and beauty. Connect with her at https://dkNaturalLuxury.com.

Holly Pitas

The Moon and the Sun

"It's not what you look at that matters, it's what you see." ~ Henry David Thoreau

Each night as I'm headed to bed I walk down the hallway and look out the window to see a perfect view of the moon. Some nights it's only a sliver, on other nights clouds create a mysterious frame. It may be the way the window glass refracts the light, but most nights, I see the light-beams of the moon stretch out into the arms of the cross.

I say a prayer of thanks for all of the wonderful gifts in my life, my husband, my family which is ever expanding into the next generation, my loving dogs, fulfilling work, my good friends and the new opportunities that will come my way. I am aware that I am blessed to live in a safe place filled with love and abundance. My life is full.

I feel like this sight of an illuminated cross is a reminder that this life is a gift, and we are to be a gift for those around us. Was I a gift to someone today? For any of my infractions, I hope to have another chance tomorrow when the day will begin with the new light of the sun.

Holly Pitas has decades of experience as both a family and a professional caregiver. She's the author of *Don't Get Caught Naked: Tips for the Adult Family Home Caregiver*, and you can learn more at www.HollyPitas.com.

Corynne Stickley

The Butterfly Effect

"Each of us has cause to think with deep gratitude of those who have lighted the flame within us." ~ Albert Schweitzer

High on a mountainside in Zimbabwe, I momentarily sensed my life's purpose. I felt alive—cloaked in the velvety darkness of the starlit night, moved to tears by this exquisite view of the universe.

Going forward, I longed to recapture that awe-inspiring moment. Why couldn't I feel it?

I protected my true inner-self while exploring many paths, searching for connection until the moment that life finally intervened.

Trusting my instincts, and hopeful for answers, I booked time to explore my internal conflict using a new technique unlike anything I knew. A unique visualization eliminated deeply hidden fears and anxiety that blocked true self-expression. With them gone, I changed. Life changed.

Can you imagine my joy at feeling connected and alive every day?

With confidence and appreciation, I began to pursue long forgotten dreams. I learned that gratitude must be heartfelt and can be as subtle as the whisper of a butterfly's wings.

After years of suppressing any desire to write creatively, I am now inspired to begin. For that, my gratitude is endless.

My deepest gratitude is reserved for Stacey K. Nye whose work lit 'the flame within' through a simple, elegant transformational technique called The F.I.X. Code. Thank you.

Corynne Stickley—educator, photographer, traveler, aspiring writer—began writing to share this unique and simple process with you or anyone seeking inspiration to change their own life. https://thefixcode.com.

Tara Kachaturoff

Grateful for Exercise

"Take care of your body. It's the only place you have to live." ~ Jim Rohn

Exercise. I love it. I've always loved it—even as a child. I grew up in a sports-oriented community in Southern California. Whether it was swimming at the Olympic-sized pool, riding my bike for miles, or playing tennis, I enjoyed being outside, moving my body and enjoying the beautiful weather year round. That early imprint created a lifelong love for physical exercise.

Over the years, my tastes in physical activities modified, and I found myself engaging in martial arts, Tai Chi, yoga, and my all-time favorite—walking.

As an adult, my love of exercise continues. I exercise daily—rain, shine, or snow! Nowadays, my routine includes yoga, assorted stretching exercises, light weights, and a lot of walking. The day isn't complete unless I exercise. While I try to get it done first thing in the morning, I sometimes split it up and do some in the afternoon.

Exercise invigorates my body, infuses it with endorphins and strengthens the connection between mind and body. It fuels me with the best energy to navigate my day—and my life! I'm grateful for the gift of exercise which has not only brought me health and wellness, but also happiness.

Tara Kachaturoff is a business coach and the creator, producer, and host of Michigan Entrepreneur, a weekly television talk show featuring businesses from startup to stellar. www.michiganentrepreneurtv.com.

Mary Choo

Gratitude's Healing Power

"Gratitude opens the door to the power, the wisdom, and the creativity of the Universe." ~ Deepak Chopra

What I love is the way gratitude gives me the feeling that someone cares and I'm not alone. As it opens my heart I feel my body chemistry changing and I start to feel more encouraged and happier inside. It gives me an inner strength to tackle whatever setback I have experienced and helps me to work out a plan B to keep me moving forward.

Gratitude for me is associated with feelings of care and kindness. It can feel like a gentle reminder to check in with myself, come back to my center and remember I don't have to do everything on my own. Maybe it's time to give myself the same care and kindness that I have received from others. Create some "me time" and practice mindfulness to calm my overwhelm and anxiety. Then I can use this space to notice the synchronicities in my life and recognize that they are silent offers of help from the Universe.

Messages that show me the Universe is always there waiting patiently to co-create with me. I just need to remember to ask, and it will bring me the help I need, often in ways I could not have imagined possible.

Mary Choo is an occupational therapist and author of "Reclaiming Ourselves." She helps people create "MeTimeSpace" and practice mindfulness to hear the Universe's messages and receive its co-creative support. Contact her at https://www.facebook.com/mindfulnessmarychoo/.

Letitia Hicks

A Heart of Thanksgiving

"I am grateful for what I am and have. My thanksgiving is perpetual." ~ Henry David Thoreau

Thanksgiving means the act of giving thanks. The Bible says we should give thanks to God, the one who created the heavens and the earth. I give thanks to God in anticipation of answering my prayers, knowing that His answers will always be in accordance with His perfect will for my life. 1 Thessalonians 5:18 states, "In everything give thanks, for this is the will of God in Christ Jesus for you." I thank God for His mercy and love for me each day.

Thanksgiving is inseparable from prayer. When I pray, I give thanks and praise God for all things. As I make my request known, I do not exclude thanksgiving. Every situation I face in life, good or bad, is a subject of gratitude and thankfulness. I always give God thanks for my daily provisions.

I give God thanks for my body, mind and spirit. I am always grateful to God for his blessings. Giving thanks to God is as natural as breathing. I have a heart of thanksgiving each day, thanking God for my family, friends, health and career. Do you have a heart of thanksgiving?

Letitia Hicks is a women empowerment strategist, entrepreneur, minster, and author. She helps to transform the lives of women with a renewed sense of power, passion and purpose. Find her at www.EvolveOutreachMinistries.com.

Karen Hannon

Be Grateful. Be Happy.

"It's not happy people who are grateful; it's grateful people who are happy." ~ Unknown

Think of a special person in your life. What word would you use to describe them? For hundreds of people in Richmond, Virginia, when they hear the word gratitude, the first person who comes to mind is Juanita Walker.

Juanita lives with a constant awareness of the gift of gratitude. She is a wise, gracious, kind, and happy woman. Juanita actually wrote a book about gratitude. Like many others, I read it and was inspired. But it wasn't until January 2017 that I made keeping a gratitude journal a daily practice.

That one simple habit has changed everything for me. I discovered that gratitude, like kindness, becomes a way that we can choose to see and walk in this world. It enriches relationships and opens our hearts and minds to the infinite possibilities that exist within each of us. So, don't wait. Start your journal today. Record five things that you're grateful for each day and see how your life changes for good.

Another, more intentional way that Juanita does is to declare a week of gratitude. Choose to do one special act of kindness that reflects your gratitude for a specific gift in your life. Watch for the miracles!

Karen Hannon is a certified Dream Builder Coach. She is living her dream by helping people realize their dreams and launching a global kindness movement. Find her at www.DestinationKindness.org.

Susan Hayes

The Business of Love

"True success cannot be measured in dollars." ~ Susan Hayes

What if your most successful year yet was when your business earned the least amount of money ever?

Well, this past year, my husband's cancer came back—stage 4. Since most of my time was spent as his caregiver, I earned far less income. This, with mounting medical bills, had left us drowning in debt. I refused people's offers for help because I should've been able to handle it, right?

As I prayed yet again for help, I saw an image of penguins huddled around one another—protecting the ones in the middle against the cold, bitter wind of Antarctica.

Penguins instinctively do what we as humans often feel guilty or "wrong" about doing. It was my husband's and my turn to be in the middle. My prayers had already been answered, but I wasn't allowing myself to receive.

With this awareness, the floodgates of abundance opened!

Where I once thought my husband's illness was "holding me back," I realized he was helping me to grow emotionally and spiritually, in a way that no amount of money could ever do, and that the most important business we are in is the business of love—giving and receiving that love.

Susan Hayes is an Access Bars with ABS, a structural energetic therapist, and a life coach who can rewire your brain, your body, and your business for success. More information: www.Facebook.com/SolActivation.

Debbie Bolton

The True Meaning of Gratitude

"Keep rocking your awesomeness." ~ Debbie Bolton

Gratitude is a feeling that reinforces within us that our lives are good and that this goodness can also be seen within others in our society. Any real act of gratitude is selfless with no intention of reward.

When we recall a memory of any situation, we re-live those emotions (but the intensity may not be the same). When we are grateful, we re-live a positive emotion within our being. Positive emotions promote both physical and emotional well-being within our own bodies.

The feeling of gratitude can be given to small or large situations. For example, my most recent moment where I felt gratitude was when I walked into my therapy room in a center and someone had put the heat on in my room. An anonymous person had taken less than a minute of their time to push a switch so both myself and my students could be warm that day (the weather had just turned colder). I am grateful for being warm.

Try this small exercise for the next week and observe the beginnings of a change within you.

Exercise: Before bedtime, write down five situations, people, or scenarios that you are grateful for that day.

Debbie Bolton is a leader in the field of alternative, complementary, and holistic therapies and an event organizer in these fields. She can be contacted via www.loveandabove.co.uk.

Metka Lebar

Gratitude for Life

"Gratitude makes sense of our past, brings peace to today, and creates a vision for tomorrow." ~ Melody Beattie

Gratitude is an acknowledgement of the perfection of life as it is in the moment. It is also the priming of the pump for even more blessings to manifest in your life. By being grateful you acknowledge your readiness to receive them. It is like saying "Thank you, life, I accept your gifts."

Try giving thanks for the things that are not yet in your life and watch the miracles unfold in front of your eyes. The universe is abundant to overflowing. Gratitude opens your heart so you are able to receive what the universe has to offer.

You can be grateful even when things are not looking so good. Be willing to find blessings in most unexpected places. If you find yourself in a challenging situation, do not resist it. Instead welcome it into your life by asking it to reveal miracles it has in store for you. Carefully unwrap the gifts hidden within adversity. By acknowledging the good in even the most challenging circumstances you can turn any situation into a blessing.

Gratitude reminds you that you are whole and complete. There is nothing that you could be missing when you embrace life with a grateful heart.

Metka Lebar is a bestselling author, visionary and consciousness facilitator who helps people activate their true potential. Read more at her website at https://www.accessoneness.com.

Rocky Henriques

"Tat You!"

"To be grateful is to recognize the love of God in everything He has given us—and He has given us everything." ~ Thomas Merton

Gratitude is not just about what has happened in the past; it also can be expressed in future tense.

When my daughter Jennifer was just a toddler and barely talking, she taught me a lot about gratitude. She had one of those little cups with a lid, so very little would spill out if she knocked it over. I was teaching her to say "Please" and "Thank you." She would come to me, drop her empty cup into my lap and say "Thank you" (though it came out as "tat you").

She fully expected me to fill her cup, and so she said "thank you" in advance. I can close my eyes all these years later and still see her doing that, even brushing her little palms together as she said it, as if she were washing her hands of the matter, leaving it all to me. That cute little habit of hers was as close to a fleshed-out example of real gratitude in future tense as I've ever seen. She had the utmost confidence that I would provide for her and take care of her need.

So will our Heavenly Father. Let us thank Him in advance.

This essay is an excerpt from *What Shape Is Your Pumpkin?: The Size and Shape of Faith*. You can find the author page for Rocky Henriques at https://amzn.to/2EMFQqZ.

Donna Mogan

My Personal Primary Caregiver

"If there are no dogs in heaven, then when I die I want to go where they went." ~ Will Rogers

When I think of my pet dog, Mystique, my heart swells with a deep gratitude for all that she taught me about unconditional loving. During several years of severe medical conditions, her loving presence could really brighten my day especially when I was experiencing pain and depression. I know it aided me in my recovery.

After a couple of long hospital stays, Mystique would jump with happiness when I returned home. Heck, there was no one else doing that.

Her antics would get me laughing and releasing all the healthy endorphins for healing. I'm convinced that the dog spit that came with all of her wet, sloppy kisses added a magic elixir that pharmacies do not provide.

When a family crisis came about, some major life changes were involved. There was a necessary move to another state, new home, community and way of life. Through them all, Mystique adapted and served as my constant personal caregiver. Many tears were buried in her fur. Yet, as usual, dog spit elixir saved the day.

Gratitude and appreciation were instilled in me by this sweet animal over our 17 years together. When I exercise them on a daily basis my life is, indeed, richer.

Dr. Donna Mogan is a life legacy, retirement and wealth coach. Her clients blend leadership, practicality and spirituality with their core values to experience new successes right now. Find her at www.drdonnamogan.com.

Bonita Bandaries

Gratitude in the Tough Times

"Give thanks in all circumstances; for this is God's will for you in Christ Jesus." ~ 1 Thessalonians 5:18 NIV

This verse had particular meaning for me during the years I was my mother's full-time caregiver. In her eighties she came to live with me after having fallen getting into her wheelchair. Nerves were damaged in her back making it impossible for her to stand or walk again.

During the years of caring for her there were many challenges to face. So, you might ask, "How can you be thankful in circumstances of disabilities and chronic illness?"

Encouraging words and deeds from family, friends, and the medical community became very important to me. Keeping a positive attitude wasn't always easy as a caregiver but taking time each day to reflect on something I was grateful for made it easier to focus on the blessings in my life. Being grateful made me more optimistic and happier as I cared for Mother. I am especially thankful for strength and guidance found in the scriptures.

I now write books and host events to encourage other family caregivers.

Bonita Bandaries is the author of inspirational books for family caregivers. Find out more at www.bonitabandaries.com.

Maria E Davis
Gratitude to Grace

"Gratitude can transform common days into thanks-givings, turn routine jobs into joy, and change ordinary opportunities into blessings." ~ William Arthur Ward

It is easier to be grateful when things are going good. How can we be grateful in the midst of pain, sorrow, illness, family or relationship drama?

Gratitude is a quality of the heart—a soothing balm to all that is out of alignment with gratitude. It promotes peace. It fuels courage to face everything that is uncomfortable.

Find something to be grateful for to prime the pump. Build on it daily. Give sincere appreciation. Think of ways to share gratitude with others. Especially to those who ruffle your feathers. Instead of complaining about what you don't like, find something you do like.

Choosing an attitude of gratitude in the face of discouragement and grief promotes healing. It opens the door to grace and endless possibilities. Knowing we cannot control others—certainly we've tried, for their own good of course! — we can choose to control ourselves and how we feel, resolve, and transcend our circumstances. What we do sets an example for others.

Gratitude is truly a gift worth giving and receiving. It lightens our load and gives opportunity to lighten others when accepted. Building a momentum on gratitude can only return blessings—an amazing grace.

Hear O Universe, I am grateful!

Maria Davis shares lifelong experiences "Keys to Overcoming Life's Irritations from the Common Cold to Crises". Take back control of your life for more energy and less disease. www. Healthrose.net

Gregory Hoffmaster

Love For One Another

"If we cannot now end our differences, at least we can help make the world safe for diversity." ~ John F. Kennedy

Gratitude is a wonderful and simple thing. Life can be much happier when I remember to remain in gratitude.

For instance, I like to remind myself to be grateful for those who came before me: those who paved the way, stood up for their rights and the rights of others. I constantly remind myself how fortunate I am to live in a place where humans of all sorts have equal rights and are safe to be their true selves. It may be just one small corner of the world, but it's a great step towards a more peaceful and tolerant planet.

I am grateful for the people who banded together, fought long and hard for equality, and faced punishments with bravery and strong hearts. Because of them, I am not only allowed to walk down the street hand-in-hand with someone I love, but I can do so safely. Though there may be some differences among us, we are all human.

We're all people who want to live life and love.

Gregory Hoffmaster is currently working (coached by Donna Kozik) on a book about social anxiety and other mood disorders. Gregory is a contributing author to Community Book Projects *Success Is Yours!* and *Everyday Joy*. Contact him at greg. hoffmaster@gmail.com.

La Wanna G. Parker

Smile and Change Your World

"One of the most rewarding things in life is to always put a smile on your face." ~ Dr. T. P. Chia

At one point in my life, I didn't know how to smile or speak to anyone if they did not speak to me first. I was also afraid to write about my feelings or stand before a group to speak, because it meant opening myself up for others to see my weaknesses.

I am so glad I made the decision to smile and say hello to everyone I met even if they did not return the greeting. It has gained me many friends I have come to love.

I have published a book sharing one of the dark times in my life. Writing *Courage to Live My Dream*, has provided me many speaking opportunities and I now share my story.

I have been blessed to make a difference in the lives of others seeking my help and it gives me great joy to see the growth in them. I am so grateful and much happier with the person I am becoming. My world changed with a simple smile and a hello. What would it take to change your world?

Thank you, God, for giving me the chance to make a difference in someone else's life.

LaWanna Parker is an author, blogger, motivational speaker, radio show host, creator of the Emerging Personal Development Program, senior citizen companion, and assistant with Project P.I.N. Blog at www.lawannaspeaks.com.

Alberta Fredricksen

Gratitude Leads to More Choice!

"None is more impoverished than the one who has no gratitude. Gratitude is a currency that we can mint for ourselves, and spend without fear of bankruptcy." ~ Fred De Witt Van Amburgh

I have often shared with friends and clients that conflict is a gift that just keeps on giving. This usually produces an animated response that leaves little room for being or feeling grateful when conflict arises. If conflict is only seen as a spoiler, a negative or something to be avoided at all costs, you lose the power of choice! Truthfully, we have good reason to choose to be grateful when conflict appears in our lives.

Gratitude is a gift and a powerful antidote to conflict or feelings of disempowerment or having no choice. If we choose to be grateful when differences arise, we can avoid engaging in power struggles.

Gratitude for what we are about to learn through exchanging information is empowering. The expansion of choice or the opportunity to decide or influence is what motivates people to go beyond their powerlessness into competence, and then from competency and confidence into achievement.

The gift of gratitude is actually a transfer of energy— of illumination, options and opportunity! We can motivate ourselves and others and offer relief from tension and inner turmoil by choosing gratitude for opportunity, and then providing choices for all.

Alberta Fredricksen is passionate about helping others transform the presence of conflict in their lives into communicating more effectively and forging stronger, more fulfilling relationships. Learn more at www.HeartPeaceNow.com.

Dawn Rafferty

An Antidote to Conflict: Gratitude

I see people who are angry. I am a mediator and a conflict management coach; in my work, emotions run high. I strive to provide a space that is calm and compassionate for potential resolutions.

Gratitude during these times is so powerful. To shine a light on things that people are grateful for in one another is often hard work, but so rewarding. Sometimes this requires reaching back in memory, to when times were good, or digging deep into the bag of common denominators, to find the appreciation. But for those who are weary of the fight, gratitude offers a graceful, healing balm.

It is scientifically proven that focusing on thoughts of appreciation, gratitude, and love brings the frequencies of our hearts and minds into coherence. We think better, we make more rational decisions, we operate from the more evolved places within ourselves.

When frustration, anger, irritation or any of the not so productive paths loom large, enumerating the things we are grateful for is a quick way home, to a peaceful heart.

Dawn Rafferty is a conflict management coach, mediator, and facilitator. She supports and guides people to better conflict outcomes. You can find her on LinkedIn at www.linkedin.com/in/dawn-rafferty.

Margy Lang

Count Your Lucky Stars

"Showing gratitude is one of the simplest yet most powerful things humans can do for each other." ~ Randy Pausch

Not long ago I was overweight, undernourished and battling an incurable autoimmune disorder. It was depressing and frustrating and led me to shun even the smallest of life's gifts.

Eventually a medical practitioner recommended I "rewire" or "train my brain" to choose healthier foods over highly processed and sugar-laden ones. Choosing healthier foods and beverages resulted in permanent weight loss and eliminated a variety of pesky food cravings.

As a bonus, I stopped the progress of the autoimmune disorder.

To support changes in my behavior I recorded my progress and setbacks. I logged the number of calories saved, hours of sleep, and minutes of exercise. Also, I jotted down what I was grateful for and how I could show gratefulness. Soon I saw the powerful connection between being grateful and healing a broken body. I titled my journal, "Count Your Lucky Stars."

At about the same time, I joined my local astronomy club and attended their observational star parties. I used my journal to record star and meteor sightings. Now when people ask me the secret sauce to losing weight and keeping it off, I tell them, "Start by counting your lucky stars."

Margy Lang is a sports marketer, author, and certified youth sports nutritionist who is completing her latest book, "500 Ways to Save 100 Calories a Day." She can be reached at margy@sportive-marketing.com.

Robyn MacKillop, Ph.D.

This Is My Life...And His

"The best way to navigate through life is to give up all of our controls." ~ Gerald Jampolsky

I wake up in the morning ready to jump out of bed and meet the day. I swing my legs over the edge and realize quickly things aren't as I expect. My legs won't swing, my body won't sit up, I can barely move. This is my morning every day now. This is my life. This is multiple sclerosis.

I struggle to find gratitude in a life weighed down by anchors I can't control so I try to focus on the floats. My biggest life preserver is my husband Don who has stood beside me through our new normal. When I struggle to get out of bed, he immediately awakens to help me. When I can no longer type, he'll take the keyboard while I dictate. He's had to take on most of my responsibilities around the house while navigating his roles as husband and caregiver.

I gave him the chance to cut the line, but he said the captain stays with the ship. He doesn't mind being the lifeboat in a stormy sea, paddling whatever direction will lead to calmer waters. He is the beacon that leads me ashore to safety. He is everything and I am eternally grateful.

Robyn MacKillop is an online course writer and savvy business owner. She is technologically advanced, fiercely independent, a lover of cats-dogs-skulls-husband, pro-education, fun and unstoppable. Find out more at http://DoctorRobynOnline.com.

Audrey Berry

World in a Soccer Ball

"Thankfulness may consist merely of words. Gratitude is shown in acts." ~ Henri Frederic Amiel

"Let's get a soccer ball--then they'll have something to play with." How do you fit a soccer ball into a shoebox? Surprisingly, it can be done if you squeeze every bit of air out and fold it flat.

Every year our family packs shoeboxes with gifts to send to children all around the world. When I stop to think about what some child I have never met might like or need, I am steered away from endless self-contemplation. Later in the year, we hear stories about where these shoeboxes have been sent. Many of the kids who get them have never received a single gift. In my world of plenty, this is hard to imagine. What wonder and excitement a soccer ball sent from a stranger far away must bring! For me, buying a soccer ball is not a big deal. But taking time to buy something for someone I will never meet changes my own heart. Though I sometimes think it's impossible to change the world, it is possible to change someone's world.

Someone's world can be the size of a soccer ball. And my world is made infinitely larger when I give it.

Audrey Berry helps disorganized moms dig out of the chaos and find workable ways to organize and run their homes. You can find her at www.justanorganizedhome.com.

Caroline Ravelo
Be Grateful for the Imperfection

"No one who achieves success does so without the help of others. The wise and confident acknowledge this help with gratitude." ~ Alfred North Whitehead

Can we feel grateful when things don't go our way?

Years ago, I was excited about a new job. I had the business, technical, and leadership experience to do well, and I was asked to write a major document for a new project.

The paper covered business process and system changes on a topic I knew well. It was initially released to a few of the senior leaders. And it was a flop!

I felt so embarrassed, disappointed, and lost.

Someone approached me and noted that I was writing for different audiences—senior leaders, middle managers, and the people doing the work. Each person would read from their perspective, and my challenge was to keep them in mind when I wrote.

She offered some technical tips, yet, the most important comment came when she asked me to overwrite. Something clicked and I reworked the entire document, which was then well received.

I am very grateful for that experience. I've shared this story with people I have mentored, managed, and led who are tasked to produce something similar. I believe we learn from others, so we can pass it on.

The gift: Be grateful for the imperfections.

Caroline Ravelo is a business architect, consultant and coach. She works with ambitious business leaders who want to implement major changes to grow their business. Contact her at Caroline@CarolineRavelo.com.

Brenda Lanigan

The Voice Within

"When you look within, you come to realize you had the answers all along." ~ Brenda Lanigan

Life can be hairy at best. In those moments when you're not sure which path to choose, if you take a moment to stop and breathe—you will find a small voice within.

When I look back over the past four months it seems surreal—the connections made, how all the experiences, people and places fit into the big picture puzzle of my life. I am grateful for listening to the inner voice of my soul; taking action, and believing in spirit to guide me in the unfoldment of my purpose.

I was forever looking outside myself for the answers. When I began taking the time to sit and listen, really listen the answers began to flow. We all have that inner voice that knows us best and the reason we chose to be here. I am so thankful I decided to be brave enough to listen and take the actions to live my purpose and love this life I have been given.

Brenda Lanigan is the CEO of The Ultimate Wellness Hub by Essence of You. Learn more about Brenda and living a preventative lifestyle at www.ultimatewellnesshub.com.

Taeko Hayatsu

Find Miracles in Your Life

"Through the eyes of gratitude, everything is a miracle." ~ Mary Davis

I have developed a track record for winning drawings and door prizes. Last year, I won a $50 gift card. Recently, I won a 40-inch TV, a book, a T-shirt, a door decoration and a $10 gift card to a local café. One of my business colleagues asked me, "Please purchase a lottery ticket for me."

How I do it? I focus on what I want to happen and I know that I am worthy of the prize. You can do it, too! If the prize is something you want, focus on it. Feel worthy of the prize. Then imagine your name being drawn.

Every day can deliver a miracle. When you go to Starbucks, maybe you are rewarded with a free coffee or tea. Unexpectedly meeting your friend at a cafe is a miracle. Do you know the probability that two people living on this planet will meet at a given moment in time?

It's so low that it is like a miracle. Take notice and say, "Thank you for this once-in-a-lifetime chance to see you and share this moment."

What is your miracle today? See it through eyes of gratitude. Notice your miracles or create them.

Taeko Hayatsu is a certified Energy Healer and Clairvoyant. She helps people clear unwanted energy, emotional dysfunctions and create space for positivity and thankfulness. Discover more at https://www.linkedin.com/in/taekohayatsu/.

Clay Morgan

The Unlikeliest of Places

"Who, being loved, is poor?" ~ Oscar Wilde

The Claypocalypse of 2009 was devastating. You may have missed it, what with no media coverage, but it was the hinge point of my life. After some bad choices and hard years, I suddenly found myself starting over in just about every way.

Maybe you've had your own apocalypse—intense loss or failure that makes life seem like a wasteland. Mine left me scraped and scarred and certain that healthy, happy relationships were as mythical as unicorns.

But like the colorful leaves of autumn, sometimes death reveals great beauty. After surviving those dark, wintry days, everything changed. I found myself 1,200 miles from the life I'd always known. New job. New city. New possibilities.

That's when I met Jen, a New York girl who met this Pennsylvania guy in Dallas, Texas. She is everything I didn't believe could be real, the happiness I didn't think could actually exist. We both kept waiting for everything to get hard and turn sour. It didn't.

I'm grateful for her, yes. But I'm also grateful for the mistakes and trials that led me to her. The Claypocalypse was terrible. And I'd do it all again if it led me back to Jen.

Clay Morgan is an author, speaker, and corporate consultant who helps entrepreneurs and creatives connect with others, speak effectively in public, and gain influence for good at www.ClayMorganOnline.com.

Ingrid Cook

Intermittent Fasting

"Health is a state of body. Wellness is a state of being."
~ J. Stanford

I never thought it was right for me and I had never tried it. Fasting. It sounded scary. Then just three months ago I heard about intermittent fasting. I was intrigued!

Did some research and reading about it, saw great testimonials and decided to try it for myself. With low blood sugar issues and some other health concerns, I was cautious but decided to start right away. It's been two months and I do love this way of losing weight, no counting calories or weighing food.

Where has this been for the last 30 years of my life? It has been fun to eat this way and to see very positive results!

I feel so blessed to have come across this and to have found great groups for encouragement and inspiration along my journey. I have come to realize it is important and invaluable to connect with others that are on your same path.

I feel I have conquered what has been a huge roadblock for me for so many years. Losing weight. This may be right for you too. Wishing you much success in your own health and wellness journey.

Ingrid Cook is a life coach, mentor, and a certified Healing Codes Practitioner for more than 12 years. If you wish to contact her, send email to Macybell@AOL.com.

Peggy Lee Hanson

My Gratitude Prayer

"The grateful mind is constantly fixed upon the best. Therefore, it tends to become the best. It takes the form or character of the best, and will receive the best." ~ Wallace D. Wattles

Dear God, Angels, Saints, Universe, and anyone else up there who runs this crazy world down here from up there: Thank you, thank you, thank you for all the blessings and events you've given me during this life of sixty-one years, three months, and two-and-a-half days, as I pen this piece.

I thank thee all for the times, as an adult, when life presented the challenges of financial strife, disappointment in knowing first hand of miscarriage, not understanding the early death of my dad, and many more instances of heartbreak.

For in not having the privilege of knowing the pains of loss, I would not know the joy of abundance, the happiness of the memories before suffering the taking away of what I held so near and dear to my heart.

Thank you, thank you, thank you for allowing me to connect with women, and men, from across the globe who share their stories and prayers of gratitude with the world that which heals hearts, calms the soul, and inspires the mind. Through my work they have permission to be who they truly are to reach those they were sent to heal, calm, and inspire.

Peggy Lee Hanson is the founder of Personal Transition Guidance, LLC. "Open up to the world and the world opens up to you." Find out more about her at https://peggyleehanson.com.

Donna Burgher

Gratitude Can Transform Your Life

"When you focus your attention on love, joy, and gratitude you will activate and attract abundance into your life." ~ Donna Burgher

Gratitude is one of the highest vibrational frequencies in our universe. When you raise your vibration to match that frequency, your life can transform.

Being grateful for what you currently have will attract more "things" into your reality, to be grateful for. This way of "Being" sends out a powerful vibration and is one of the secrets to creating and manifesting your desires.

An attitude of gratitude creates a powerful, positive mindset. In a world that seems topsy-turvy, it may be a challenge to find things to be grateful for.

Focus on the good, the gifts, and the blessings. This will create an energetic shift, that can have a positive impact in your life and in the world.

Parents who inspire their children to focus on gratitude will see a positive shift in their kids. It is less likely that they will become selfish and self-entitled when they show appreciation for what they have.

The energy of gratitude fills your heart with love and joy. And, when you feel grateful, you will want to be kind and helpful to others.

Living in the energy of love, joy, and gratitude can transform your life.

Donna Burgher empowers and inspires parents and kids to Create, Attract, and Manifest™ their desires, so they can enjoy and love their lives! To learn more, visit www.DonnaBurgher. com.

LuWanda Ford

Reaching Out Toward Gratitude

"Gratitude is our most direct line to God and the angels...The more we seek gratitude, the more reason the angels will give us for gratitude and joy to exist in our lives." ~ Terry Lynn Taylor

When times are tough it is hard to think of feeling grateful. Family members are estranged and there is serious illness in a loved one.

You are dealing with the passing of a family member though you were not close but have to handle the final affairs and distribution of the belongings. It is hard to feel gratitude for anything.

You can wallow in the darkness of depression and wonder, "Why me?" Pressing through that depression and making the effort to list what you are grateful for is a difficult exercise but it is valuable if you can force yourself to do it.

Start with the little things. You woke up this morning. You can walk on your own. You know family and friends are praying for you. You have food to eat. These seem like such small things but it can start turning you toward gratitude.

Stretch a bit further. Who values you? Who treats you with respect? Who do you know who cares about you?

Listing those people turns the tide. It starts you thinking about happier times and you have made the turn around the bend to gratitude. Your day will be brighter for this.

LuWanda Ford is small business builder who shows people how to earn money while teaching them to be as healthy as they can be. Find her at https://luwanda.reliv.com.

Tonia Sample

Today, I'm Grateful

"Gratitude is when memory is stored in the heart and not in the mind." ~ Lionel Hampton

My sister died. My beautiful, spirited, gifted sister. I'm filled with sadness, disbelief, but also gratitude.

I'm grateful for her spark, it not only ignited me, but everyone around her.

I cry tears over her death, but I'm also reminded of the tears shared in laughter, and that beautiful smile.

I am grateful that she lived a life full of passion, and left a beautiful impression on this world and our hearts.

Yes, today I'm grateful. Even as my heart aches, I know these are not only tears of loss, but tears of gratitude...

Tonia Sample is an author, speaker, entrepreneur, and life coach. She can be reached at sunny14life@aol.com.

Julaina Kleist-Corwin

The Story Changed

"Gratitude is the ability to experience life as a gift. It liberates us from the prison of self-preoccupation." ~ John Ortberg

My mood instantly changed from happy to down with just a few words.

Sundays are my marathon reading days. It's my favorite activity. Last week I started a book and couldn't put it down. It's philosophical with well-crafted characters and a continuing hook. Due to commitments, I had to stop reading with 50 pages left.

This Sunday I picked it up again but the character's mindset changed. The aging protagonist agonized over a scathing letter he wrote as a young man to his best friend, severing their bond. His friend committed suicide a year later. Now he couldn't overcome remorse.

The protagonist surmised that life isn't all it's cracked up to be. Wham! My mood dropped.

I hoped he would recover by the end, but I didn't find out. I closed the book.

Every day, I am filled with gratitude for all life. That protagonist's disregard for the precious gift he had, stopped any further enjoyment of his story.

During my morning walks in nature, I express my love for life, for people, animals, plants, the sky, the earth, and for the light that is within us. "Gratitude promises forgiveness," I told the protagonist.

Julaina Kleist-Corwin is a teacher and story consultant who shows people how to improve energy levels from stuck to success. Contact her at jmkcorwin@gmail.com.

Kit Rosato

Best Birthday Gift Ever

"Of all God's gifts both great and small, children are the best of all." ~ Unknown

The day you were born was magical. Steady, early contractions were keeping me from sleeping. Needing a distraction, I decided to polish my beautiful silver platters that were badly tarnished from neglect. I hate polishing silver but it seemed like a good idea at the time. Your dad happily went to sleep while I slaved away.

Hours later we were in the hospital walking the halls to encourage progression in my labor. You were coming a week early, and I was so grateful to be having you naturally without drugs. Your precocious brother had been born C-section 18 months earlier. It was also the day before your dad's birthday.

My labor was long and I was so exhausted from polishing the silver that I struggled to push you out. The clock struck midnight and your dad whispered to me that I didn't need to wait any longer. You were going to be his best birthday gift ever! Hysterical at the crazy idea I had been waiting to deliver on his special day, his words renewed my strength.

With grateful hearts and God's perfect timing we welcomed you, our beautiful daughter, on your dad's birthday.

Kit Rosato is an online entrepreneur who loves helping others, writing, selling on Amazon, and taking the mystery out of online marketing. Connect with her at https://KitRosato.com.

Cherry-Ann Carew

No Limits to Being Kind

"Kindness is contagious." ~ Unknown

You've most likely seen the quote "kindness is contagious" in a meme on the Internet, or heard it in conversation. And it's true on the giving and receiving front.

The beautiful thing about being kind is that everyone benefits. Because we all appreciate when people are nice to us, these actions motivates us to keep paying it forward in varying ways.

It could be using our voices to convey meaning. Talking is the way the majority of us prefer to communicate, so telling an employee they're doing a fabulous job, or, calling a friend to let her know that she's not forgotten will release "feel good" chemicals to boost your mood.

Maybe you like writing. If you do, send an email, text message or a hand-written note card thanking your co-worker for helping you finish a project on time. Write an inspirational note for your child. Leave a positive blog comment for the blogger whose article helped you solve a problem or gave you a million-dollar idea.

Consider these ways of giving back through your words or other forms of language. There are truly no limits to the ways we can be kind to one another.

Cherry-Ann Carew is an Amazon multi-bestselling author and online business strategist. She helps new online business owners simplify the online biz maze. Visit her website http://cherryanncarew.com to find out more.

Adrienne Dupree

I Can Make a Difference Because of Her

"All I am or ever hope to be, I owe to my angel mother." ~ Abraham Lincoln

A young 16-year-old girl in love with her high school sweetheart learns that she is pregnant and must suddenly make adult decisions. This is the 1960s, so continuing to attend high school is not an option and she drops out. She decides to not only have the baby, but to keep it.

This is not some drama from a Lifetime movie, but a story about my life. I am the daughter that my teenage mother decided to have and keep. I can only imagine how scared she was. I know when I was 16, I wasn't ready to face adult responsibilities.

My parents ultimately got married and raised me and my three siblings. I am so grateful that she decided to keep me, raise me and love me unconditionally. Growing up I didn't really realize the sacrifices she made for me. She sacrificed her education and teenage years for me. The significance of this selfless act didn't hit me fully until I became a parent myself.

Even though my mother is no longer here, it's my mission to show my gratitude to her everyday by being the best person I can be.

Adrienne Dupree is an entrepreneur who teaches people how to get out of the rat race. You can find her at http:// LeaveTheCorporateWorldBehind.com.

Anne Domagala

Evan's Canyon at First Light

"When you rise in the morning, give thanks for the morning light." ~ Tecumseh

There is a trail called Evan's Canyon at the north end of Reno, the start of many miles of the Nevada landscape owned by Bureau of Land Management. A trail runner could get lost up there, and for this I'm grateful.

There is no light like the pale salmon pink that takes the horizon at dawn. The bowl of Reno dotted with buildings and trees stretches toward the base of the Sierras, adopting the new hue of daylight. The temperature is cool, the air tinged with the scent of earth and sage. I am grateful for the morning light, for the muscles and breath that carry me up the winding narrow clay trail of Evan's Canyon, first along the creek and past the owl that turns his slow gaze toward me, then up past boulders and scrub to the vista overlooking the city.

I'm grateful for the dog that has accompanied me for years along the top of the canyon, the constancy of earth, the surprise of California quail alighting from behind a stone. I am reminded that I am a breathing human running along a tiny bit of land mined for precious metal, and that this is precious earth.

Anne Domagala is a writer, illustrator, and international finance professional living in Oakland, Calif. Find out more at www.drawinginthemargins.com.

Warren L. Henderson, Jr.

Gratitude in Rising Up

"He alone sees truly who sees the Lord the same in every creature...seeing the same Lord everywhere, he does not harm himself or others." ~ Krishna Quotes from *The Bhagavad Gita*

One summer morning in 2012, I joined with several prison ministers gathered at Donovan prison in San Diego County, California, to hear recognized community leader Father Greg Boyle address about 300 inmates. Many of us had read Father Boyle's book, "Tattoos on the Heart." Everyone in attendance was moved.

A dozen ministers then met offsite and began planning an organization that would duplicate Boyle's Los Angeles work in San Diego. Over the following months we met to brainstorm and form a business plan.

Gratitude is expressed in our vision statement: Building communities of kinship that recognize the value and strength of every member by providing services offering hope, support, counseling, education and, job opportunities. We strive to coordinate community partnerships to facilitate a comprehensive integrated approach to eliminate the conditions that lead our youth to join gangs.

We are grateful for graduates of Rise Up Industries and their work in developing and refining our re-entry program. They serve as role models and peer mentors for newer members following in their footsteps.

Warren L. Henderson's experience includes 40-plus years as an engineering consultant and college professor. His books and lectures are based on community involvement, including prison ministry, inter-faith groups, and others. WarrenHCL@ hotmail.com

Ruth Strebe

Cookies of Love

"Sometimes the smallest things take up the most room in our hearts." ~ Winnie the Pooh

Gina dutifully embarked on a quest to integrate gratitude into her daily habits. "I'm thankful for the inventor of toothpaste" she told herself as she brushed. "I'm thankful that I have two legs to walk on" she told herself as she tied her shoes. But it didn't feel real. This gratitude felt like an academic exercise in alternate theories.

Gina decided on a different approach. She made some tea, curled up in a soft throw and mused about past gratitude. There were some biggies, like the time her boss traded cars with her. But she kept coming back to Nat.

Back then Gina was an overwhelmed single mom. At Girl Scouts one night, her daughter reminded her that she needed cookies for something the next day, and Gina just sagged with exhaustion. Nat, one of the other moms said "I can make some cookies for you tomorrow if you want. You can stop by and pick them up on your way to the event."

Gina and Nat became good friends for years. Later their families went separate ways, but Gina's heart swells with gratitude every time she thinks about those cookies of empathy and years of friendship from Nat.

Ruth Strebe works with companies experiencing trouble with efficiency, productivity or employee experience by helping them find and solve the root of these issues. www.linkedin. com/in/ruthstrebe

Katie De Souza

Enjoy Every Moment

"Life is made of small moments like these." ~ Above & Beyond

The breeze gently blows through the window swaying the curtain letting the sun shine onto my face, signaling the beginning of a new day. I stretch. Turn to glance at the clock. No alarm. I do not need alarms anymore.

I am grateful to wake up when I want. I choose what I will do each day. I have organized my work so I have time to enjoy life. Walking down the road, I see squirrels running around collecting acorns and leaves for their den, and birds flying overhead with worms in their mouths to feed their young.

Sometimes the house is a mess, with dirty dishes left in the kitchen; however, I appreciate each moment.

I enjoy a hot cup of tea with my daughter, in-between replying to emails. I like chatting with my son whilst he explains the latest game he's playing, in-between planning our next event. These are special moments I cherish.

I once only had 30 minutes for lunch, and I was told when to take it. Now lunch with my parents for as long as I want.

Sit down and decide what you truly want. Then create a plan—make it happen. Create your own magical moments.

Life really is what you make it.

Katie De Souza is an author and entrepreneur who inspires couples to achieve their dreams and live a happy and fulfilling life together. Find out more at www.katiedesouza.tv.

Gabby De Souza

Be You – I'm Me

"Today you are you. That is truer than true. There is no one alive who is you-er than you." ~ Dr Seuss

I am grateful that my parents made me go to the gym because I needed to go.

I remember one of the first times I went to the gym, I looked in the mirror and I saw a podgy 14-year-old and I wanted to cry. Now I cry if I don't go to the gym.

I used to run past the mirrors to avoid them. Now I workout in front of them.

I feel really comfortable there. It helps with my mind. I feel calm and relaxed. I love the endorphin rush.

Sometimes your demons are your best friend. I confronted going to the gym. What once was uncomfortable and unknown is now pleasant and enjoyable. I feel at home at the gym. I am happy and grateful I discovered the enjoyable benefits of exercise—by stepping outside my comfort zone.

Fast forward a few years and I now know how important your health is. I value being healthy more than anything.

Gabby De Souza is an avid gym goer who loves keeping fit. When she's not at the gym she's creating beautiful logos and artwork. Find out more at www.gabbydesouza.co.uk.

Suzanne Cousins

Light Up a Life

"Gratitude is a currency that we can mint for ourselves and spend without fear of bankruptcy." ~ Fred De Witt Van Amburgh

I had a wonderful childhood with lots of laughs, fun and happiness. Later in life I married and had two wonderful daughters and grandchildren—a life that would be envied by many. I will be forever grateful to my parents, brothers, husband, children and grandchildren for the happiness in my life.

After 40 years of marriage my husband decided he wanted someone other than me in his life and I was absolutely devastated. It was one of the lowest points of my life and I found it very difficult to cope. But life is full of ups and downs and we have to find ways of travelling through the downs to come up the other side again.

My coping mechanism was my wonderful Spaniel dog Millie. She was there for me when I needed her, a friend and companion. The love and loyalty of a dog is endless, and I can't express the gratitude I felt for my little friend. She saw me through the devastation and travelled with me to the up side again. Gratitude works both ways and she knew happiness from her gratitude to me. Thank you, my friend, for being there and bringing me happiness again.

Suzanne Cousins has created a group on Facebook to help people realize there is a life after divorce, called Sparkle after Divorce. https://www.facebook.com/groups/SparkleAfterDivorce/

Melissa Ellen Penn

Body Wisdom

"Gratitude runs as an undercurrent through human experience at its most vibrant, always and everywhere." ~ David Steindl-Rast

There is a great blessing in becoming older and to see the ripeness of wisdom moving out, through me, as an evolving gift. Often I hear the words of past teachers flowing from me into the hearts and minds of my students—as they once moved from Source through countless tongues and cultures that came before.

Humanity is struggling mightily to move itself, through gratitude, into the heart of compassion. Often it seems like we, collectively, are losing our way, and this necessary task is but folly. It is in these moments I turn to my senses. I gaze at the beauty of the turning leaves, orange and russet against the grey of the sky. I hear the cacophony of the wild geese overhead—their great "V" piercing storm-filled clouds on their way home. My skin prickles in the wind; cold as it blows off the snowy slopes of the Rockies. I smell the smoke from my neighbor's chimney and remember the fires from of my past.

Gratefully I sip strong, black tea from a hand-hewn cup while feeling the smooth glaze under my fingers. I smile in remembrance of the friend who gave this gift to me to honor my birth, and sigh.

Melissa Ellen Penn is a spiritual director and teacher of ethics for individuals and businesses that wish to be exceptional. More at https://www.linkedin.com/in/melissa-ellen-penn-educator/.

J. Russell Burck

From Duty to Gratitude

Who is gratitude for?

My mind doesn't remember how I reacted when my parents asked, "Did you say thank you?"

My body said, "Shoulders collapse toward the sternum, chest tenses, throat tightens to squelch a scream, 'I hate that question.'" Grati-duty.

Gratitude was for my parents.

Now, what is gratitude for?

Coaches recommend: "Write down three (or five or ten) things you're grateful for."

"Don't repeat items." Gratitude as chore?

"Morning and evening. Watch what happens."

Gratitude fosters personal growth.

Or, gratitude can benefit your business.

Gratitude counts because it's useful.

What does authentic gratitude feel like?

My body remembers how I felt when I prayed with patients as a hospital chaplain-intern. I started my prayers, as I still do, with "We give thanks that you are with us all the days of our lives. If we're in the Valley of the Shadow, you are there. You make us glad that we can lift up our concerns, our complaints, our fears just as they are."

Peaceful, safe, loved.

Duty-to-thank has become gratitude. Gratitude has become awareness of abundance. Awareness of abundance becomes expecting good in all things.

What a great path!

Russell Burck, retired hospital chaplain and ethicist, is an intuitive reader and healer who helps physicians recover joy in treating people. Find him at http://russellburckconsulting.com.

Louise Lavergne

Gratitude Ritual to Transform Your Life

"If the only prayer you said in your whole life was 'thank you,' that would suffice." ~ Meister Eckhart

The word ritual implies an established set of procedures to mark a special occasion or ceremony. The Thanksgiving dinner ritual is one that we are all familiar with. A ritual is like a prayer in motion. It elevates your intention into something meaningful and healing. Just like Thanksgiving, it is non-denominational.

A ritual requires three things:

1) Intention: For example: "To create more peace in my body & in all areas of my life now."
2) Focus: Redirecting your mind to focus on your intention and stay present for the duration.
3) Effort: Set a time and space and make this important enough to give it your full attention.

As you allow yourself to soften and ease into gratitude an amazing thing happens - you feel good. Not just about yourself but about everything and everyone.

Remember to take time to breathe in gratitude to live in joy.

Louise Lavergne is an author and spiritual teacher of personal growth and empowerment.

She gives guidance and inspiration so you can become the healer of your life. Get her free gratitude guide at https://www.foundation4yourlife.com/pl/49483.

Katrina Oko-Odoi

Growing in Gratitude

"There's a party inside of me that's celebrating everything I do." - Clifford Oko-Odoi

I've learned most of what I know about gratitude from my husband Cliff. When we met in our twenties, we had tons of fun but shared a cynical outlook on life. Gratitude as a practice wasn't on our radar.

Two years later, I was in graduate school and Cliff was working full-time in sales while finishing his degree. Then he got fired. This single event paved the way for a new chapter in our lives. While unemployed, Cliff dedicated himself wholeheartedly to self-reflection and improvement. He read countless books, developed daily affirmations, and over time profoundly changed his outlook on life to one of positivity and gratitude. I was skeptical. But as I watched him grow into a more fulfilled and optimistic person, I started believing in a positive mindset too.

As Cliff has taught me, it all comes down to gratitude: being grateful for where you are right now *and* for what is to come. I began my own journey of gratitude thanks to his example, and our children and business emerged from this shared mindset. I am incredibly grateful for Cliff, our sons, and the life that we've built. I look forward to continuing to grow in gratitude.

Katrina Oko-Odoi is a published author, PhD, and Founder & Chief Editor of ContentWorm, a company dedicated to content marketing, writing, and editing for businesses and entrepreneurs. Learn more: www.contentworm.com.

Our Favorite Causes

The contributors of *The Community Book Project: A Gift of Gratitude* proudly stand by these non-profit organizations and encourage you to find out more about them and donate if so inspired.

Alexandria's House

www.voaspokane.org/alexandrias-house

Teen pregnancy can trap homeless mothers and their children in poverty and domestic violence. Alexandria's House provides a safe, supportive and nurturing home for expectant and new teen mothers.

Alzheimer's Foundation of America

www.alzfdn.org

The Alzheimer's Foundation of America (AFA) mission is to provide optimal care and services to individuals living with Alzheimer's disease and related illnesses and to their families and caregivers.

American Cancer Society

www.cancer.org

The American Cancer Society is a nationwide, community-based voluntary health organization dedicated to eliminating cancer as a major health problem.

Asheville Mushroom Club

www.ashevillemushroomclub.com

Since 1983, the Asheville Mushroom Club has been dedicated to members' education on all things fungi and to finding and recording mushrooms found in the mountains of western North Carolina.

Beloved Women Organization

www.belovedwomenorg.com

Beloved Women Organization is a humanitarian Christian women's organization that serves women regardless of religion, race, or ethnicity.

Best Friends Animal Society
www.bestfriends.org
Best Friends Animal Society runs the nation's largest no-kill sanctuary for companion animals and building effective programs that reduce the number of animals entering shelters.

Chasing Daylight Animal Shelter
www.chasingdaylight.org
Chasing Daylight Animal Shelter offers a brighter tomorrow for pets and their people. The mission of CDAS is to protect animals from suffering and cruelty with a primary emphasis on providing care for domestic cats and dogs until "forever homes" are found.

Chestnut Mountain Ranch
www.cmrwv.org
Chestnut Mountain Ranch provides a Christ-centered school and home for boys in crisis and in need of hope and healing. Partnering with their families, they pursue family restoration and reunification.

Community Development Resources
www.CDR-Nebraska.org
It is the mission of Community Development Resources of Nebraska to create economic opportunity and strong communities by providing capital and technical assistance to develop and fortify small businesses.

Community Partnership Family Resource Center
www.cpteller.org

Community Partnership Family Resource Center (CP) in Divide, Colorado, supports families and children by focusing on strengths and providing free resources to change lives for the better.

COTA

www.cota.org

The Children's Organ Transplant Association (COTA) helps children and young adults who need a lifesaving transplant by providing fundraising assistance and family support.

Crossroads Relief and Development

www.crossroads.ca/relief-development

Crossroads Relief and Development gives tangible support to people through food and water, rescue and care, and health and education.

Donors Choose

www.donorschoose.org

Donors Choose makes it easy for anyone to help a classroom in need with the goal of moving closer to a nation where students in every community have the tools and experiences they need for a great education.

Dream Fetchers

www.dreamfetchers.org

Dream Fetchers brings persons and animals together to interact and bond, offering a wonderful distraction from pain, depression, hopelessness, or frustration; which it believes helps promote healing and well-being.

Dress for Success

www.dressforsuccess.org

Dress for Success empowers women to achieve economic independence by providing a network of support, professional attire and the development tools to help women thrive in work and in life.

Facial Pain Association

www.fpa-support.org

The Facial Pain Association supports persons suffering from Trigeminal Neuralgia (considered the most painful afflictions known to medical practice) through support groups and the International Light Up Teal Night.

First Coast No More Homeless Pets

www.fcnmhp.org

The mission of First Coast No More Homeless Pets is to end the killing of shelter cats and dogs in northeast Florida, southeast Georgia, and across the nation.

Garden Organic

www.gardenorganic.org.uk

Garden Organic spreads the word of an organic future and healthy planet for all. They protect heritage seeds and train communities and individuals in growing and composting.

Gift of Life

www.giftoflife.org

Gift of Life believes every person battling blood cancer deserves a second chance at life—and they're determined to make it happen. They're singularly passionate about engaging the public to help get everyone involved in curing blood cancer, whether as a donor, a volunteer or a financial supporter. It all begins with one remarkable person, one life-changing swab and one huge win—finding a match and a cure.

Gilda's Club Chicago

www.gildasclubchicago.org

Gilda's Club Chicago offers free programs for men, women, children, and their families and friends whose lives have been impacted by any kind of cancer.

Global Health Ministries

www.ghm.org

Global Health Ministries of Minneapolis brings medical equipment and supplies to enhance and sustain the health and well-being of some of the most vulnerable people on earth.

Graines d'Avenir

http://www.grainesdavenir.com

Graines d'Avenir (translated 'Seeds of Future', a French charity) supports Tibetan children in exile to be educated in their culture, provides humanitarian, educational, medical and logistical assistance to Tibetan, secular and religious communities, to disadvantaged non-Tibetan local populations as well as to diverse populations of Buddhist culture.

The Guide Dog Foundation

www.guidedog.org

The Guide Dog Foundation offers increased independence and enhanced mobility to people living with blindness, low vision, or other disabilities by providing them with expertly trained guide and service dogs.

Heifer International

www.heifer.org

Heifer International helps families achieve self-reliance and pass this gift to others. It gives animals to families and then teaches them sustainable farming practices. The family extends the gift by passing on the first female offspring of their livestock to another family.

Help a Mother Out

www.helpamotherout.org

Help a Mother Out works to improve baby and family wellbeing by increasing access to diapers for families in need. Access to a reliable supply of clean diapers reduces the risk of infectious disease outbreaks, improves babies' health and comfort, and enables babies' participation in early care and education programs.

KCRM

www.KCRM.org

KCRM is a Christ-centered community offering freedom, hope and resources to the poor and homeless, along with those struggling with addiction, to empower them to reach their full potential.

Keep Punching

www.keeppunching.org

Keep Punching's mission is to knock brain cancer out for the count, by raising money for brain cancer research, and for funding patients' needs. Keep Punching offers hope, comfort, and a positive outlook to others during a hard time, while relentlessly fighting to prevent and eradicate brain cancer.

King Hussein Cancer Foundation

www.khcc.jo/en

KHCF is the largest community-based organization in Jordan dedicated to combating cancer. KHCF's work focuses on fundraising and development, global advocacy, public awareness on early detection and prevention, cancer coverage and patient support.

Knit Your Bit

www.nationalww2museum.org/programs/knit-your-bit

The National World War II Museum hosts Knit Your Bit events for creation and collection of handmade scarves. The scarves are distributed to veterans nationwide. Free patterns are available online.

La Jolla Golden Triangle Rotary Club

www.lajollagtrotary.org

The La Jolla Golden Triangle Rotary Club, with membership including more than 100 local business leaders, helps the local community and has service projects in over 30 countries.

Leukemia and Lymphoma Society

www.lls.org

The mission of The Leukemia & Lymphoma Society (LLS) is to cure leukemia, lymphoma, Hodgkin's disease and myeloma, and improve the quality of life of patients and their families.

Lighthouse Foundation in Australia

www.lighthousefoundation.org.au

The Lighthouse Foundation in Australia provides homeless young people from backgrounds of long-term neglect and abuse, with a home, a sense of family, and around-the-clock therapeutic care. Through the experience, young people can heal, learn again to relate to others and start to rebuild their lives.

Little Princess Trust

www.littleprincesses.org.uk

Little Princess Trust provides real hair wigs free of charge to children and young adults who have lost their own hair due to cancer treatment and other illnesses.

Luv Way Ministries

www.luvway.org

Based in Los Angeles, Luv Way Ministries works to improve the lives of abandoned and orphaned children in Kenya.

Lydia's Love

www.lydiaslove.org

Founded in 2011 in memory of Lydia Greer, Lydia's Love provides birthday celebrations for homeless and underprivileged children.

Mary Elizabeth's Ministry for the Homeless

www.memfth.com

Mary Elizabeth's Ministry for the Homeless mission is to seek out those living on the streets and provide the basic needs to the homeless through their community outreach.

Music for the Soul

www.musicforthesoul.org

Music for the Soul creates CDs and DVDs that tackle life's toughest issues to bring healing to the hurting soul. In ministry to women, these resources penetrate hearts deeper than any words can convey.

Network for Grateful Living

www.gratefulness.org

The Network for Grateful Living is a global non-profit online sanctuary that invites visitors into a way of living imbued with gratitude. It offers online and community-based educational programs and practices.

Operation Christmas Child

www.samaritanspurse.org/what-we-do/operation-christmas-child

Operation Christmas Child's mission is to provide children around the world with shoeboxes filled with small gifts as a means of reaching them with the Good News of Jesus Christ.

Ovarian Cancer Circle
www.theovariancancercircle.org
Mission: to create an ever expanding ring of networking, education and support for women of all ages, their extended families and friends who are affected by ovarian cancer.

PAWS
www.pawsweb.org
The Performing Animals Welfare Society (PAWS) is dedicated to the protection of performing animals, to providing sanctuary to abused, abandoned and retired captive wildlife, to enforcing the best standards of care for all captive wildlife, to the preservation of wild species and their habitat and to promoting public education about captive wildlife issues.

PBS
www.pbs.org
The mission of PBS (Public Broadcasting Service) is to create content that educates, informs, and inspires. Contributions ensure the health of an important community resource.

Pelican Harbor Seabird Station
www.pelicanharbor.org
Pelican Harbor Seabird Station is dedicated to the rescue, rehabilitation, and release of sick, injured or orphaned brown pelicans, seabirds, and other native wildlife; and the preservation and protection of these species through educational and scientific means.

Plan International

www.plan-international.org

Plan International is an independent development and humanitarian organization working in 71 countries across the world to advance children's rights and equality for girls.

Pocket Flag Project

www.pocketflagproject.com

The Pocket Flag Project supports US deployed and deploying troops with a "little piece of home" they carry in their pockets. It is a small US flag folded in the traditional triangle shape. Since its founding in 2001, over 2.8 million flags have been sent to volunteers all over the US to fold and send to troops.

Project P.I.N. (People In Need)

Contact: chyrell.english@crusadersoffaith.org.

Project P.I.N. distributes food to people in need.

Rise Up Industries

www.riseupindustries.org

Rise Up Industries minimizes gang involvement by providing integrated gang prevention, gang intervention and post-detention reentry programs.

Ronald McDonald House Charities

www.rmhc.org

Keeping families with sick children together and near the care and resources they need.

Rotary

www.rotary.org

Rotary is a global network of 1.2 million neighbors, friends, leaders, and problem-solvers who see a world where people unite and take action to create lasting change – across the globe, in our communities, and in ourselves.

San Diego Humane Society

www.sdhumane.org

San Diego Humane Society is a non-profit animal welfare organization committed to ending animal homelessness.

ShareLife

www.sharelife.org

ShareLife is a Catholic charity supporting agencies that carry out the mission work to serve the most isolated and vulnerable people in greater communities.

Sleeping Children Around the World

www.scaw.org

Sleeping Children Around the World is a 100 percent charitable global community of volunteers and partners who have transformed the lives of over 1.5 million children in developing countries by providing bedkits for a good night's sleep.

Society of St. Vincent de Paul

www.svdpusa.org

The Society of St. Vincent de Paul, a Catholic lay organization, leads women and men to join together to grow spiritually by offering person-to-person service to those who are needy and suffering in the tradition of its founder, Blessed Frédéric Ozanam, and patron, St. Vincent de Paul.

Talk It Up TV

www.talkituptv.com

Talk It Up TV helps make the world a better place through life-changing acts of kindness for those in need.

Timothy's Gift

www.timothysgift.com

Timothy's Gift is a non-profit organization that provides inspirational programs in prisons in multiple states, focusing on bringing hope to inmates and staff. It shares a transformative message of hope and of the intrinsic worth of every human being, regardless of their past or their current situation.

Unity Foundation

www.unityfoundation.org

Unity Foundation promotes world peace, cooperation and unity. The organization produces the Peace Day Global Broadcast Celebrating the UN International Day of Peace and Positive Spin TV.

USO

www.uso.org

The USO strengthens America's military service members by keeping them connected to family, home and country, throughout their service to the nation.

Utica Baptist Church

www.uticabc.com

"The church with a sweet Spirit" is more than just a motto for Utica Baptist Church in Utica, Mississippi. This congregation in the Deep South truly demonstrates its love for Christ through loving and serving others.

Wilderness Awareness School

www.wildernessawareness.org

Wilderness Awareness School is an internationally-recognized leader in outdoor education. They help children and adults cultivate healthy relationships with nature, community and self.

World Vision

www.worldvision.org

A Christian humanitarian organization helping children, families, and their communities overcome poverty and injustice.